aircraft illustrated
ANNUAL 1986

£4.95

aircraft
illustrated
ANNUAL 1986
Edited by Peter R. March

LONDON

IAN ALLAN LTD

First published 1985

ISBN 0 7110 1509 0

© Ian Allan Ltd 1985

Published by Ian Allan Ltd, Shepperton, Surrey;
and printed by Ian Allan Printing Ltd at their works
at Coombelands in Runnymede, England

Contents

All photographs *Peter R. March* unless otherwise credited.

Cover:
Spitfire IIA of the Battle of Britain Memorial Flight.

Left:
Lightning T5 flying from the A&AEE in 1984.
MoD(PE) A&AEE Photographic Group

Previous page:
The second prototype Olympus-engined Vulcan VX770 shows the original wing configuration in this take-off shot. *Bristol Aeroplane Co*

Thirty years of Friendship

Alan J. Wright

Windmills, cheese, canals, tulips and clogs — just a few of the obvious things for which Holland is famous. Less obvious perhaps but just as important is the Dutch aerospace industry with its much envied reputation and success record and that means Fokker.

Founded in 1919, Fokker has always been particularly involved in the design and production of various airliners. In fact at one point before WW2, over half of the world's civil transport aircraft originated from the Dutch company. A close association with Douglas became evident in 1935 when the European manufacturing and marketing rights were obtained for the DC-2 and DC-3, both then extremely modern and at the beginning of long careers.

The occupation of Holland in the spring of 1940 brought the company to a halt. During the war years some work was carried out for the Germans, but it was of a very minor nature proving of little value to either party. In any case the attentions of the Allied air forces meant that the workforce spent more time on building repairs than on production. As the war progressed so the number of attacks increased, until by 1945 most of the Amsterdam factory had been destroyed.

It was 1951 before a new complex was built at Schiphol, but in the immediate postwar years, the company had designed and built several different types including the S-11 and S-12 basic trainers, the twin engined S-13 and the S-14 Mach Trainer.

Some time had already been spent by the design team on investigations into possible airline requirements, particularly for a DC-3 replacement. Of course Fokker was not alone in this field since a good many other manufacturers had their eyes on this potentially lucrative market. Because over 60% of the traffic on routes of up to 1,000 miles was carried by the type, there seemed to be hope for everyone to get a share.

A medium sized machine was therefore proposed which would be capable of carrying about 32 passengers in a pressurised cabin. Considerable thought was given to its power-plant. Turbojets and turboprops were already in and advanced stage of development for civil aircraft, while the well proven piston engines then available were considerably more reliable than their prewar counterparts. However, eventually it was decided that twin Rolls-Royce Dart turboprops had more to offer than the alternatives.

As in the UK, a government board had been set up in Holland to plan the future of the country's aviation industry generally. Known as the Nederlands Institut voor Vliegtuigontwikkeling, it was approached for authorisation to proceed with the project. Once received the serious and detailed design work for the new airliner commenced. The F-27 Friendship had been born.

While much of its energies went into the creation of its own product, the company was also kept busy not only by maintaining numerous DC-3s and other types, but also in the production of Gloster Meteors. Work on military contracts has continued through the later generations of fighters from Hunters and Starfighters to the modern General Dynamics F-16 of the present day.

The configuration chosen by Fokker for the new airliner was one much favoured by the company in its prewar designs. A high wing was considered to be safer in the event of a wheels-up landing, the fuselage absorbing the sudden contact with the ground rather than wings and engines. For this it had to be strengthened, but it was thought to be worthwhile in order to reduce the possibility of fire and the inevitable damage to expensive powerplants. Commercial advantages included the faster turn-rounds that could be achieved due to easier ground handling and the unobstructed downward view enjoyed by most passengers. Even those travellers disliking the sight of a wheel disappearing into an engine alongside them could at least appreciate the absence of glare from the unpainted wings.

Top:
After serving as the prototype Friendship, PH-NIV was finally withdrawn in 1962. *Fokker*

Above:
Aer Lingus was an early operator of the F-27; EI-AKG, seen here landing at Bristol Airport, was used until 1966.

Simultaneous with the aircraft taking shape in Holland, back in the UK Rolls-Royce had been developing the Dart and was now in a position to offer a much improved version. This allowed Fokker to revise the F-27's performance estimates and at the same time comply with the requests of several potential customers by extending the fuselage by three feet. Although not incorporated into the prototype PH-NIV, subsequent machines were built with the new length as standard.

Appropriately the first firm orders for the new airliner came from the Dutch flag carrier KLM, although it was largely a gesture to help launch the production run. Unexpected, but none the less very welcome, was the attention paid by the small American operators. Such was the interest in the Friendship, that the Fairchild Corporation decided to produce the type at its Hagerstown plant, for which purpose a licence was awarded. The company also acquired the sales rights for the whole of North and South

America, the only exception being Brazil where Fokker was already established.

Thirty years ago, on 24 November 1955, the F-27 left the ground for the first time under the control of Fokker test pilot H. V. B. Burgerhout. The 34min flight of the unpressurised and unfurnished prototype was uneventful so it was able to embark immediately upon its test programme. Very few changes were found to be necessary during the course of the development flying, the only significant modification involving the flaps. Tests at maximum weights proved to be better than expected bringing a marked improvement in landing and take-off distances. Pressure testing was carried out at Schiphol using the second airframe in the water tank, following which it was employed for further structural trials with and without pressurisation. Once successfully completed, the fourth airframe took over the final stages of the flight simulation programme.

During the whole of 1956, all flying had been the responsibility of PH-NIV, but on 31 January 1957 relief came with the arrival of the second

prototype, registered PH-NVF. Unlike its partner it was finished to airline standard since it was also intended to be the company's demonstrator, enabling the marketing team to display the aircraft much more effectively than hitherto. Its delayed availability was due to late deliveries of equipment which, together with detailed design refinements, meant that 'India Victor' was forced to carry the burden alone longer than orginally intended. It is interesting to note that while this machine was honourably retired in 1962, its companion is still in airline

Above:
The F-27-100 VH-CAT has served in Australia since 1959. *Alan J. Wright*

Below:
The second prototype F-27 is still flown by the German carrier DLT on its internal services; it is now registered D-BAKI. *Alan J. Wright*

Below right:
Air Anglia became the first operator of Friendships in the UK, its fleet reaching 10 before becoming part of Air UK. *Alan J. Wright*

service with the German domestic carrier DLT using the identity D-BAKI.

Across the Atlantic the American prototype first flew as N1027 on 12 April 1958, to be joined shortly after by the second on 23 May. They differed from the European version in having a longer nose to accommodate weather radar while not surprisingly much of the internal equipment was now supplied by US companies. Integral stairs were also incorporated into the passenger door and the fuel capacity was increased by some 400 US gallons.

Such was the effort that Fairchild was able to deliver its first production aircraft in August 1958, enabling West Coast Airlines to operate its initial service out of Seattle on 28 September. Other carriers were soon able to follow as the F-27s flowed from the Hagerstown factory. In Venezuela, Avensa commenced operations on 3 October from Caracas, while later that month, the Friendship was introduced to its Montreal schedules by Quebecair.

In Europe the first customer outside Holland was Aer Lingus whose order had been placed on 29 March 1956. Almost two years later, on 23 March 1958, the company's first example was flown wearing the test registration PH-FAA. Upon delivery on 19 November 1958 it took up its intended Irish marks of EI-AKA. After a period of route proving and demonstration flights, the Friendship began to carry fare-paying passengers on 15 December between Dublin, Glasgow and Liverpool. By this time three aircraft were on strength so very soon afterwards the Manchester, Bristol, Cardiff and Birmingham sectors were added to the type's routine trips.

Fokker designated these early examples as the Mk 100. Powered by two Dart 511s, the variant was available with interiors laid out for up to 48 seats with baggage space of up to 240cu ft, although no underfloor holds were provided. Higher operating weights were made possible by the Mk 200, the second version of the F-27 to be offered. This time the more powerful Dart 528s were installed, but otherwise it remained similar to the earlier model, becoming a very popular choice with operators. It remained in series production until March 1971, but even after this Fokker was prepared to produce it to order if specified by a customer, particularly since there was always a shortage on the second-hand market.

Air UK, as the largest operator of the Friendship in Britain, has found this to be a problem on occasions when needing to increase its fleet size. For this reason a pair of 100s was acquired, one of which had been partly built to 200 standards, so in due course it proved a relatively straightforward and worthwhile operation to convert it by replacing the engines. A similar change for the second machine proved uneconomic, but it has subsequently continued in service alongside its uprated colleagues. Strangely enough it is the fleet favourite amongst the crews principally because it is quieter and slightly faster.

Logically the Mk300 came next and was again based on the 100 series, differing in having a large forward cargo door and strengthened floor. Few of the 13 built were sold to airlines, most of them entering service with No 334 Squadron of the Royal Dutch Air Force at Soesterberg. These Troopships, the name by which they are known, have faithfully operated in their transport role for many years, during which time they have shed their bright civilian style livery for sombre grey/green camouflage.

Occasionally the type performs energetically at an air display, trailing smoke while engaging in gyrations far removed from those normally expected from such an aircraft.

Naturally the Mk 200 received similar treatment to emerge as the 400 series. It too had the passenger/cargo availability of the 300 but had the added benefit of the Dart 528s. Amongst the world's airlines, this version has proved very popular in areas where there are seasonal variations in traffic. Carriers can adjust the ratio of the freight/passenger mix according to day-to-day requirements. As the 400M, the model becomes a military transport equipped with two rear dispatch doors for paratroops or supply dropping. In this guise it can carry 45 fully armed troops using the customary side-slung canvas seats, or alternatively five tons of freight. Both rear doors are opened manually at about 100kt for the benefit of those wishing to leave before the aircraft reaches the ground, their departure assisted by the downwash from the high wing. A range of 950 miles is possible with such loads. Conversion into an ambulance is easily carried out, resulting in two rows of 12 stretchers arranged in four tiers of three.

Most airliners are subjected to a stretching exercise at some point in their careers and the F-27 is no exception. Fokker added 4ft 11in (1.5m) to the fuselage, bringing the seating capability of the Mk 500 up to a maximum of 56. One particularly good feature of the F-27's cabin dimensions — however long the fuselage — is the impracticability of squeezing in seats five-abreast. It therefore retains the comfortable pairs along each side of the centre aisle

Left:
Destined for Angola, PH-FSK a srs 500, revealed its large cargo door at Farnborough 82. *Alan J. Wright*

Below left:
A pair of US-built Fairchild-Hiller FH-227Bs were used by Skyways for a short time for freight and passenger work. *Alan J. Wright*

Above:
A familiar sight at airshows is the smoke trailing, low-flying F-27-300 Troopship of the Royal Netherlands Air Force.

wherever it is in service. Again the 500 has military applications, but the majority have found homes in civilian hands. Air France has found the type especially valuable on its postal contracts, the schedules for which are far from easy. With a door sill of only 3ft 6in (1.06m), heaving mail bags in and out becomes less arduous even for a short Frenchman.

Introduced in the late 1960s, the Mk 600 was basically a 200 series aircraft provided with the forward cargo door, but without the strengthened floor of the 400. It attracted a fair number of orders and has continued to be produced at a steady rate. Two projected versions designated the Mks 700 and 800 were not built, the former being a 600 series with the lower rated Darts of the 100/300 range, while the 800 had a rough field undercarriage but instead became known as the 600RF.

Through the years Fokker has maintained F-27 production at a fairly steady level, peaking at 3.5 units per month at one point but averaging around the 1.5 mark. On the other hand 6.5 aircraft per month rolled off the American line to meet a rash of orders only to dry up by 1969. Well before the end, the manufacturer, by now trading as Fairchild-Hiller, had announced its intention to offer a stretched version subject to receiving a minimum of 30 advance orders.

Mohawk Airlines went a long way towards satisfying this requirement by opting for 18 of the model in preference to modernising its Convair 440 fleet with turboprops. Taking the identity of FH-227, it still retained the familiar F-27 configuration but had grown 6ft (1.83m) longer thereby accommodating a maximum of 56 passengers. It was not long before other carriers such as Northeast, Piedmont and Ozark followed the example set which ensured the airliner's launch. Eventually 78 were built, serving for some years with their original owners before passing to smaller operators around the world. This includes Europe where the largest collection is to be found in France in the hands of the domestic carrier Touraine Air Transport (TAT). The type has never been common in the UK, although two were used for a short time by Skyways before the demise of the company in 1980.

Throughout its long career the Friendship has been available for military use. However apart from some target towing and photographic work, the aircraft has generally maintained a sedate existence as a troop or freight transport. A mildly aggressive nature was planned for the variant introduced by Fokker in 1976. Intended for coastal patrol, shipping surveillance or search and rescue, it was given the title of F-27

Maritime. An ex-Turkish Air Lines Mk 100 (TC-TEK) served as the prototype, although production examples are based on the 200/400 series. A forward mounted ventral radome houses the scanner for the search radar, while the two observers amongst the six crew members are each provided with an observation blister which replaces the normal windows. With additional fuel supplied by centre wing or pylon tanks, the machine's range is increased to over 2,000 miles.

Although this version was not intended to carry weapons, the Royal Thai Navy does operate three armed specimens. However in 1984 Fokker announced the existence of the new Maritime Enforcer which from the outset was designed to carry out its duties in a far more belligerent manner than any of its predecessors. For this role the aircraft is armed with a variety of missiles, gun pods, a lightweight torpedo, searchlight or fuel pod plus rocket and flare launchers. To assist in the effective use of all this hardware, nose, belly and tail radars are installed. Internally the crew's stations are much more sophisticated than those of the earlier Maritime model as could be expected. This anti-submarine and surface vessel machine has already attracted much interest and is expected to be sold in some numbers. After all, the F-27 was aimed to be a DC-3/C-47 replacement all those years ago, so if the latter can be a gunship why not its successor!

Also new from the Dutch company is the F-27 Sentinal. Essentially it is a border surveillance and stand-off reconnaissance aircraft designed to monitor possible hostile activities across frontiers. The radars carried provide the ability to spot the movement of large vehicles as far as

80 miles (150km) distant. As a high flying camera platform in the relative safety of friendly skies, the threat of anti-aircraft fire is removed in times of conflict. Sorties of this nature can be carried out discreetly in peacetime to produce the same results, but without the embarrassment of international incidents.

Another radar-equipped F-27 proposed by Fokker has been christened the KingBird. It awaits definite orders before a go-ahead is given, but the company is hopeful that delivery could follow in about 2½ years from that time. As an early warning aircraft it could fill a dangerous void in many countries' defences, particularly those unable to afford a Boeing 707 AWACS and all that goes with it.

Despite providing the platforms for these three new military adaptations, the Friendship is nonetheless an elderly design. In the face of growing competition from new generation projects such as the ATR42 and British Aerospace ATP, to remain a force in the international market Fokker needed either to give its thoroughbred airliner a major facelift or introduce a brand new product. Apart from the prohibitive costs arising from the latter option, there really were few improvements that could not be incorporated into a development of the original well proven airframe. This reasoning led to the Fokker 50 which was duly launched in November 1983.

Originally updating work planned for the F-27 was restricted to a straight change from Darts to the Pratt & Whitney PW100 range of engines. While bringing improvements in performance, it did little for the passengers apart from reducing the cabin noise level by a few decibels. From the feed-back from possible customers it was quickly found that it was not enough. However there seemed little demand for a machine of significantly increased capacity,

so 50 seats were taken as the basic number, hence the new designation. When required the cabin size does permit a maximum of 58 fitted at a 30in pitch four-abreast. In length the fuselage is virtually the same as the F-27-500, but thought has been given to a future stretch to give a capacity of 66 seats. Passengers will benefit from a new ventilation system, but are more likely to notice the 21 small square windows which ensures that all 15 rows of seats are adjacent to at least one. No doubt the passing of the large oval variety will be mourned by some, since like those on the Viscount they seem to represent an era in air transport now sadly gone. Following the current policy

Above:
Internally the Fokker 50 carries on the standards set by the latest Friendships. *Fokker*

adopted for the latest F-27s, the interior has the modern large capacity luggage bins above the seats giving it the so-called 'wide-bodied look'. Once again there are no under-floor holds, baggage and cargo being carried in areas fore and aft of the cabin.

The other major external difference concerns the powerplant. Twin Pratt & Whitney PW124s have finally been selected which will give the Fokker 50 a cruising speed of up to 30kt greater than the Dart-powered F-27. Even if the new shape of the nacelles fails to be noted, the unusual sight of the Dowty Rotol six-blade propellers should raise an eyebrow. Traditionally passengers have always used the port side rear entrance door on the F-27. Although still present, it will be employed for galley work and servicing, while the customers will embark via a forward door equipped with airstairs. Provision has been made for a large freight hatch, if required, in a similar manner to its predecessor.

Naturally the flightdeck has not been forgotten and it is here that full use has been made of the latest technology available. Designed to reduce the pilots' workload, the instruments have been arranged to give optimum readability by tilting the panels by 10 degrees. Cathode ray tubes (CRTs) are installed in front of each pilot for altitude and horizontal situation displays, replacing the normal electro-mechanical types. Space has been left on the centre pedestal for a

fifth CRT which if necessary can be used for weather radar. Alternatively navigation data and checklist information can be displayed.

With the design frozen, by mid-1984 tooling and detail production was well underway with a target for the start of final assembly in March 1985. Dates have tended to drift a little from those originally planned due to a lack of positive orders despite a genuine interest by operators. Slower than forcasted economic recovery from the recession of the 1970s has been largely responsible, with budget conscious airlines giving greater priority to their main-line jet fleets before turning to short-haul requirements. At least the consequences of the hesitancy have been shared by all the manufacturers.

A glut of regional airliners have either appeared or, like the Fokker 50, are well advanced. For this reason it will not be an easy market in which to succeed, but the Dutch machine will have the advantage in coming from such a reliable type as the F-27, production of which will continue for the foreseeable future. Deliveries of the new airliner are scheduled to begin in July 1986, subject to its first flight the previous November and a successfully completed test programme. Perhaps in 2005 it will assume the appropriate name of Friendship 50!

Russell Adams — photo ace

Roger P. Wasley

Roger Wasley invites famous aircraft photographer Russell Adams to choose some of his photographs and presents a brief biography of this camera ace.

Asking Russell Adams to select just a handful of favourite air-to-air photographs to illustrate his own work is demanding a lot. The former chief photographer of the Gloster Aircraft Co took many thousands of superb photographs during his 20 years with the company and Hawker Siddeley. And it doesn't take a professional cameraman to appreciate the quality and scope of this vast photographic collection.

Mr Adams is known as the man who pioneered air-to-air photography of high-speed jet aircraft during the late 1940s and early 1950s. His original and imaginative approach to a difficult task was acclaimed across the world and inspired a host of now famous photographers who followed on. But his illustrious career began almost by accident. Mr Adams was an electronics engineer• in the Research Department at Gloster's when, in May 1949, he was asked to photograph excessive skin deformation on the rear fuselage and tail-fin of a Gloster Meteor.

The photographs he took of the aircraft from the backseat of another Meteor T7 flying alongside proved so useful and so dramatic he was asked to fly more technical sorties. As word of his pictures spread, so requests for his work increased. He made history when he produced the first air-to-air aerobatics pictures of a jet aircraft — Meteor WL364 in a loop.

In 1952 Mr Adams won the coveted First Award in the descriptive category of the British Press Pictures of the year competition. More than 1,500 pictures had been submitted by 179 press photographers. The winning picture showed the second Hunter prototype WB195 being put into a vertical climb by Hawker's chief test pilot Neville Duke. It was taken by Mr Adams flying alongside in a Meteor T7 flown by test pilot Brian Smith. The following year he was made a Fellow of the Royal Photographic Society after he submitted a selection of air-to-air photographs.

Demand grew for his work and for years he was regarded as the world's leading aerobatics cameraman. Mr Adams had a passion for aerobatics and his breath-taking assignments included photographing the forerunners of the *Red Arrows*, the *Yellowjacks* from No 4FTS, Valley with their Gnats; the Central Flying

Left:
Russell Adams posing with one of the cameras he used during his flying years with Glosters in front of a Javelin FAW9. *Roger Wasley*

School's Meteor T7 team and the *Red Pelicans* with its Jet Provosts; the Meteor F8 team of No 500 Squadron, Royal Auxiliary Air Force; the Vampire FB5 team of No 501 Squadron, Royal Auxiliary Air Force; the Hunter team of No 41 Squadron and, of course, the *Red Arrows* when the team flew Gnats from Kemble.

To carry out his pioneering work in the air he had to overcome many obstacles — the main ones being wearing glasses and the weight of the plate cameras he used in the early days. His Speed Graphic plate camera normally weighed 6½lb, but during high-speed aerobatics it had a weight equivalent to 20lb or more.

Mr Adams faced and overcame many demanding challenges during his exciting and hectic years with Gloster's and Hawker's, but the results he achieved, as illustrated in a small selection of his photographers on these pages, were well worth the effort. They are a lasting tribute to a dedicated professional.

This picture:
Jet Provost T3s from the CFS high over the Cotswolds, one of Russell's favourite backdrops.
Russell Adams

Right:
Four Gloster Javelin FAW1s of No 46 Squadron in echelon starboard on a flight from Odiham in 1957.
Russell Adams

Below right:
A good deal of pre-flight planning was required for this unique sortie of CFS aircraft flying from Little Rissington in 1954. A Sabre F4 is leading a Canberra B2, Meteor NF14 and Meteor T7. *Russell Adams*

Left:
Hawker test pilot Neville Duke loops the second prototype Hunter WB195. The photo was taken from the backseat of a Meteor T7 flown by Brian Smith, who managed to stay with the Hunter round the loop.
Russell Adams

Left:
Photographing in the loop was repeated in 1955 with this classic shot of a formation of Hunter F1s from No 54 Squadron in box formation. *Russell Adams*

Top:
Russell Adams did not restrict his subjects to jet fighters. This pair of Argosy transports of No 114 Squadron were caught on a sortie from Benson in 1962. *Russell Adams*

This picture:
Hawker Siddeley Trident 1 G-ARPB banks to starboard on a test flight from Hatfield in 1962. *Russell Adams*

The Luftwaffe's Pirates

Ken Wakefield

Thursday, 6 March 1941 was a wet, wretched day. A persistent mist kept visibility down to something like 2,000yd for most of the afternoon and a lowering cloud base with drizzle threatened to bring on an early dusk. However, it was still light in the Bristol area when the city's air raid sirens were heard at 7.03pm that gloomy evening.

Barely had the last moan of the sirens subsided when a low flying aircraft appeared over the northern outskirts of the city. Disregarding the city's barrage balloons, which were barely visible in the miserable half-light, the raider dropped a stick of seven high explosive bombs and machine-gunned streets and roof-tops as it climbed back up into cloud to make goods its escape to the south. It left behind, in the Southmead district of Bristol, 15 seriously damaged or destroyed houses, a wrecked Baptist church and about 400 slightly damaged houses. One person was killed, six seriously injured and nine slightly hurt.

Once more, a 'hit and run' or 'sneak' raider had struck, providing, as the newspapers of the day recorded, 'another example of Nazi brutality, another case of an indiscriminate attack on the civil population'. But such was not the intention of the attacker. Nor, apparently,

did the crew of the German bomber think that they had achieved such militarily feeble results for, acting on their report of events, the attack was hailed in the German and Italian press as an outstandingly successful attack against the factories of the Bristol Aeroplace Co at Filton, on the outskirts of Bristol. The German bomber — a Heinkel He111 of Kampfgeschwader 27, commanded by Oberleutnant Hollinde and crewed by Oberfeldwebel Lebuda, Unteroffizier Weber and Gefreiter Schilling — had indeed passed low over Filton, but the entire bomb load had missed the intended target and achieved only the results here described.

The attack was typical of many being carried out at this time by low flying aircraft, operating singly and taking advantage of low cloud and poor visibility to avoid fighter interception; but not all were so unsuccessful. Only a week or so before, on 27 February, a single German bomber had carried out a low level attack on the Parnall Aircraft Co factory at Yate in Gloucestershire, causing severe damage and 87 casualties. Such operations, flown by crews selected for their skill and experience, were officially termed *Zerstörangriffe* (pinpoint destruction attacks), but were better known to Luftwaffe crews as *Pirateneinsätze* or 'pirate' attacks.

The first pirate attacks took place while the Battle of Britain was still at its height. One or two crews in each Staffel were chosen for these special missions which were recognised as potentially very hazardous; in addition to the threat posed by barrage balloons and light machine guns, there was the danger of inadvertently flying into high ground or other obstacles in the poor visibility and low cloud that such missions demanded. A cloud base of 800-1,000ft with not less than 8/10th cover and visibility of about 2,000yd, together with extensive solid or layered cloud up to about

Left:
Feldwebel Martin Reiser, an observer (navigator/bomb aimer) with 9/KG55, in the nose of an He111 during a low-level pirate operation in 1940.

22

10,000ft, provided almost ideal conditions and crews were specifically ordered to abort and return to base if better conditions were experienced.

The approach to the target — and aircraft factories figured high on the priority list — was usually made at medium altitudes (5,000 to 10,000ft), flying in cloud or between layers and navigating by radio methods. This included the use of Knickebein VHF beams and the MF (medium frequency) radio beacons located on enemy-occupied coasts from Brest to Norway. Approaching the target area, a descent was initiated over safe, low ground, to establish visual contact with the ground. This was a hazardous procedure over Britain where, in really poor frontal conditions, even moderately high ground is covered by cloud, and precise radio altimeters had not then been introduced. Having established their position — and usually a well defined landmark was chosen as an initial aiming point — a low level approach was made to the target. Whenever possible, railway lines were chosen as a lead-in guide, and often the approach run was flown at a very low altitude, sometimes as low as 20ft. The actual bombing, however, was normally carried out from 100 to 1,000ft, using bombs fitted with short time delay fuses (Type 25) which allowed them to enter buildings before exploding. The short delay also enabled the aircraft to escape damage from its own bombs. After bombing, cloud cover was again sought for the return flight to France or the Low Countries.

Pirate operations brought with them a new recognition for bomber crews. Until now,

unlike their fighter pilot colleagues, they had largely fought their war under a cloak of anonymity. Not for them had been the glory and the public adulation afforded to fighter pilots — Mölders, Galland, Wick, Machold and others were almost household names; as their 'kills' increased, so did their prestige and fame, so it was with some pleasure that bomber crews read the Wehrmachtbericht — the daily war communiqué — issued to the German public on 28 September. Herein was mentioned the name of Oberleutnant Leonhardi in connection with a low level attack on a factory in the Midlands. Two days later the Wehrmachtbericht continued the new trend with the report of a successful attack on another Midlands factory, this time carried out by Oberleutnant von Butlar and his crew. At last, or so it seemed to many German bomber crews, their own branch of the services was getting the publicity which was its due.

By the first week in October 1940, with weather conditions favouring pirate operations, attacks had been attempted on a number of factories and airfields, but results were very often at variance with the claims. However, some concern was felt in Britain defence circles because of the difficulties in countering such attacks. The weather conditions effectively prevented fighter interception and the low attack heights limited the effectiveness of

23

Above:
Hauptmann Johann Speck von Sternberg, the Staffelkapitän of 9/KG55 (centre), with his crew at Villacoublay prior to take-off for a pirate mission.

Right:
The word *Pirat* (pirate) can be seen on the engine nacelle of Hauptmann Speck von Sternberg's He111P2.

anti-aircraft defences — only light anti-aircraft guns, such as the Bofors and the Hispano, were effective antedotes and there was a serious shortage of these weapons.

Successful low level attacks on a factory in the Midlands on 4 October were claimed in another Wehrmacht communiqué, the credit for these going to Oberleutnant Neumann and Leutnant Bischoff, commanding to Junkers Ju88s of KG77. Three days later accolades for more successful attacks against targets in the south of England went to crews under the command of Oberleutnant Braun, Oberleutnant Biemar, Oberleutnant Kühn and Oberfeldwebel Wolf, but by no means were the attacks as successful as claimed — navigational errors and inaccurate bomb-aiming produced very different results.

Martin Reiser, an observer (navigator/bomb-aimer) Oberfeldwebel serving with 9 Staffel of Kampfgeschwader 55 (9/KG55), flew his first pirate mission on 15 October 1940, his pilot and Staffelkapitän being Oberleutnant Speck von Sternberg. A second operation of this type four days later was aborted, however, when only $\frac{1}{10}$th cloud was found over the English coast. Under no circumstances were pirate missions to be continued with less than $\frac{5}{10}$ths cover so, with Portland Bill in sight while en route to the Bristol Aeroplane Co factory at Filton, von Sternberg turned back to Villacoublay where he landed with four 250kg and eight 50kg bombs still on board his He111.

On 24 October, Reiser flew his third *Piratenflug* — coincidentally his 24th operational flight over Britain — and upon his return wrote the following account of the mission which, again, was intended against the aircraft factory at Filton, Bristol. And again, his pilot was Oberleutnant von Sternberg.

'"Pirate crew prepare for a mission!" was the call at the close of the Staffel briefing. So, we climbed into our flying overalls, put on our fur-lined boots and gathered up our flying helmets, oxygen masks, navigation bag and life jackets and climbed into the truck that was to take us to the Operations HQ. There we donned our parachute harnesses and made our way to the aircraft where Oberleutnant von Speck and an official Luftwaffe War Correspondent named Kirchhoff awaited us, the latter flying on this occasion as gunner. Our target was to be the aircraft factory at Filton which we had already attacked on two occasions by night. But today it was bright daylight with a layer of cloud at about 5,000ft above us, a useful cover for our approach to the target. It would have been insane to attempt our flight with less cloud and thereby inviting the attention of the Spitfires and Hurricanes.

'As the entrance hatch was closed in the belly of our He111, I cast my eye over the bomb load stowed in the bomb bay section of the fuselage — four 250kg and four 50kg high-explosives. What a shame, I thought, that we could not take more with us, but we needed a fair amount of petrol. The motors came to life, the brakes were released and we rolled out to the take-off position. As we did so I checked the ammunition magazines for my MG15, checked the switches on the bomb release selector and set the first course on the compass. At the take-off point the motors were opened up to full throttle and we were on our way. After about 45min we were over the French coast, passing over radio beacon "Willi" situated at Cherbourg and flying above the cloud layer at a height of 1,400 to 1,600m (about 5,000ft). Take-off was at 12.50hrs (11.50 British time) and at 13.02 British time we crossed the English coast, navigating by means of Knickebein and D/F bearings on radio beacons. We flew a direct course from Cherbourg to the target.

'After flying over England for about 10min there was a large gap in the cloud and through it I recognised Bath, to the south-east of Bristol.

We continued over land and then came into more cloud. All the crew were now fully alert and at their positions for action. Looking down through an occasional hole in the cloud it was difficult to accept that we were over enemy territory — we could see peaceful meadows, orchards, roads with cars moving, a dual railway line and a small town with a river running through it. And then we were in cloud again. "We had better turn around" said the Kommandant, but I replied with a reminder about the extent of the cloud. "Who knows how far we are from the target?" he retorted and I replied that I had pin-pointed the small town on my map and we hadn't far to go. After seven minutes I reckoned we were over the aircraft factory. But we were still in solid cloud, so we went down. The altimeter started to unwind. 1,000, 900, 800, 700m — and at last we were free of cloud. We had turned to the south and now to our right the water of the River Severn glittered. Beneath us was green countryside with a railway line, and then Oberleutnant Speck called out, "Airfield to the left; there are hangars", and he banked to the left while pulling the release handle to position the Visier sight for lining up on the target. He rocked the machine, a sign that the bombs were going in a single "stick". Meanwhile I had already selected the right-hand lever so that the entire load was released. Then, from the *Bodenwanne*, the ventral gun position, the flight mechanic called from his prone position "Hangars and buildings hit!" Then a new call, nearly in unison with machine gun chatter — "Fighter behind and to the right!" The crew members in the rear opened up with their MG15s while Oberleutnant Speck zoomed our machine back up into the cloud. After a while we came down lower again, but the fighter reappeared and again we had to go into the cloud.

'We re-crossed the Channel, where there was now only about half cloud cover, and looked down at the rough sea, hoping that the motors would keep humming away nicely because we didn't relish the thought of an involuntary bath in the icey water. Further south we reached the French coast, which was covered in cloud. We had to get a bearing from our ground station, but no course correction was necessary and finally we touched down at our home airfield. We then made our report to the Gruppenkommandeur who was most pleased with the outcome of our trip and offered us cigarettes.'

This operation was carried out in a Heinkel He111P that carried the markings G1+FT. As on the outward flight, the return was made via radio beacon 'Willi', the aircraft landing back at Villacoublay at 15.25 BST.

There is no doubt that the crew of this aircraft were certain that they had successfully attacked their assigned target, but in fact no bombs fell on or near Filton on 24 October. A low flying German aircraft did, however, drop eight HE bombs at Yatton, between Bristol and Weston-super-Mare, at 13.37hrs on the day in question. This agrees very closely with Martin Reiser's log, which gives a bombing time to 13.40 (14.40 German time), and there is no doubt that the Yatton bombing was carried out by the G1+FT. The main GWR Bristol-Taunton railway line was blocked by the crater of a bomb that fell in the centre of the track. One bomb failed to explode, but the remainder straddled the track around Yatton Junction. Relief lines were opened to traffic after six hours and both main up and down lines were open again two days later. No casualties occurred.

It seems fairly certain that the HE111 emerged from cloud just south of Bristol, having slightly overshot the target, according to Reiser's calculations, and Speck, looking out to his left, mistook the railway for the line running past Filton. Mistaking the buildings and sheds around the junction for the aircraft factory — and in the short period of time they were in sight such a mistake is understandable — the attack was hurriedly carried out with the results here described.

Bad luck dogged the same crew a few days later when poor weather conditions again prevented them finding their assigned target which, once more, was the aircraft factory at Filton. Taking off from Villacoublay at 12.45hrs G1+FT followed the same route (via beacon 'Willi' at Cherbourg) but this time carrying four 250kg and eight 50kg bombs, all fitted with special low altitude fuses. The English coast was crossed at a height of about 5,000ft but because of dense cloud the Heinkel flew around in a large circle, climbing to 12,000ft. However, icing conditions were experienced and Ober-leutnant Speck von Sternberg descended again to about 8,000ft. Still in cloud, course was set for Filton, Martin Reiser navigating by means of back bearings on the 'Willi' beacon. Approaching the target a descent was initiated, the He111 finally breaking cloud at a very low height. Then, flying at a height of only 60 to 100ft, the German crew sought their target, but without

success. As they roared across the countryside people waved to them, no doubt thinking it was a British aircraft, and horses and cattle, startled by the roar of their engines, scattered. And then, at last, a large factory came into view and without hesitation an attack was carried out, the aircraft opening fire on men wearing white overalls. The entire bomb load was dropped on the factory and buildings and other installations were claimed to have received hits. Damaged railway installations were also seen as the Heinkel turned away and disappeared into the cloud at about 100ft. The climb was continued to 6,000ft, returning on a direct track to Villacoublay where a landing was made after a flight of 4hr 10min duration.

In a subsequent Wehrmachtbericht the destruction of a factory near Bristol was claimed, but in fact no bombs at all fell in the Bristol area that day, nor indeed did any bombs fall anywhere in the South-West Civil Defence Region which included Gloucestershire, Somerset, Devon, Cornwall, Dorset and Wiltshire! Among other places, however, bombs were reported in South Wales and the Midlands, but damage was only slight and there were few casualties.

In many ways this attack was typical, but German claims continued to give the impression of success after success. In the Wehrmachtbericht of 4 November Hauptmann Storp of II/KG76 was credited with outstanding achievements in attacks on airfields and other important targets in London, but the greatest publicity yet was afforded to a crew that carried out an attack on an aluminium works at Fort William in Scotland on 23 December. An aircraft commanded by Oberleutnant Fidorra and crewed by Leutnant Mündel, pilot, Oberfeldwebel Botha, wireless operator, and Unteroffizier Lemberg, gunner, was stated to have pressed home its attack in spite of heavy flak. Explosions and smoke were seen by the crew and the outcome of the attack was beyond doubt. Subsequently the issue of *Der Adler* magazine for 25 February 1941 featured an article on the attack. Printed in several languages for worldwide distribution, the article was illustrated with drawings by the well-known Propaganda-Kompanie artist Ellgaard whose work was a regular feature of the German flying magazine. However, like most pirate operations, although some damage was caused the extent and seriousness claimed by the Germans was grossly exaggerated.

Oberleutnant Friedrich Rinck, the Staffelkapitän of 9/KG30, was an ambitious man with an outstanding personality. An enthusiastic and experienced operational pilot, Rinck set a magnificent example to the crews under his command. In 1937 he was seconded to the Hungarian Air Force and spent some time in Budapest training Hungarian pilots on He45 and Do23 aircraft. Upon his return to the Luftwaffe he was posted to 1/KGr100 at Köthen, from where he took part in long training flights to Tripoli and the Canary Islands. Rinck had formerly been a flying instructor at A/B, C and Blind Flying Schools, but at the outbreak of war he was employed on operational duties. He took part in the Polish and Dutch campaigns and was also involved in attacks on Dunkirk during the evacuation of the British Expeditionary Force. Then came day and night attacks on British targets and towards the end of January 1941, he completed his 99th operational flight. His 100th 'Feindflug', he decided, called for a special celebration and accordingly he approached his Gruppenkommandeur with the request that he be allowed to carry out a special pirate attack to mark the event. The request was granted, though it was not usual for permission to be granted to Staffelkapitäne to undertake such missions.

Rinck's first pirate attack had been in September 1940. On that occasion his target consisted of two large hotels in Harrogate which were believed to be occupied by the Air Ministry. His first attempt to destroy these hotels was aborted when the cloud base was found to be too high. A few days later a second attempt was thwarted, again by a lack of cloud cover, but the third proved more successful. The clouds were at 3,000ft and a stick of three 500kg bombs was dropped. The first appeared to score a direct hit on one hotel, the second fell in a roadway destroying a passing car and the third appeared to fall wide.

The target selected for Rinck's 100th mission was a factory at Grantham in Lincolnshire, believed by the Germans to be the only factory in Britain making Hispano-Suizea cannon for aircraft. A report on this factory, supported by photographs, was allegedly received from an agent in November 1940, and in consequence an attack was laid on and, it was believed, the factory destroyed. However, another agent's report indicated that there was a new factory, adjacent but on the other side of the railway line passing close by, and it was this complex that was now to be destroyed. Two aircraft were to participate, the second being under the command of Leutnant Dahlmann.

Rinck's aircraft was 4D+CT, a brand new Ju88-A5 (Works No 2280) making its first operational sortie. His crew consisted of Obergefreiter Ernst Stiller (bomb-aimer), Oberfeldwebel Wilhelm Reuter (wireless operator), and Unteroffizier Ferdinand Wissing (gunner). The crew was non-standard in that a bomb-aimer (*Bombenschutze*) and gunner (*Bordschutze*) replaced the more usual observer (*Beobachter*) and flight mechanic (*Bordmechaniker*), but this was becoming increasingly common by early 1941 as losses in 1940 and the need for quick replacement lowered the standard of training given to German aircrew personnel.

The two Ju88s departed Amsterdam/Schipol on the afternoon of 27 January, a cold, grey day offering apparently ideal conditions for pirate attacks. During the flight visibility was down to little more than one mile, and visual contact was maintained below the low cloud ceiling. Landfall was made just north of Great Yarmouth and the aircraft then skirted the coast to Boston, where the coast was finally crossed at 1,300ft. Several AA gun positions were seen,

but no fire was encountered. Oberleutnant Rinck had no difficulty in finding the railway line running west from Boston through Sleaford, and followed this to Grantham. At the point where the line curved to the left, with the old factory on the left-hand side, Rinck carried straight on to attack the new building. To his surprise he came upon two factories — where photographs had led him to expect one — but undaunted he prepared to carry out his attack.

The AA batteries at Boston had not opened fire and in view of this Rinck felt confident that his aircraft had not been tracked by the British defences. He therefore came in to attack in a leisurely fashion at 500ft and received something of a shock as the light AA defences guarding the establishment opened fire. Nevertheless, four bombs were released, rear-gunner Ferdinand Wissing subsequently reporting that two appeared to score hits, damaging at least one of the two buildings comprising the factory.

As soon as the bombs were released Rinck turned for home, but already, he noticed, oil was leaking from the port engine. This engine soon began to vibrate and with temperatures soaring it was shut down and feathered. An inspection of the port wing revealed numerous hits and clearly the aircraft was in bad shape. The Ju88 began to lose height and by the time it reached Boston it was below the level of the highest ground. When it became apparent that the aircraft would not clear the next line of trees along its track, a forced landing was made.

The first and last operational flight of the 4D+CT — and Rinck's 100th — terminated at 15.30hrs in a field at Tilley's Lane, near Boston. Rinck made a good belly-landing and the crew, none of whom was injured, then destroyed the aircraft, using the 3kg cannister of explosives fitted for the purpose. This made a sound job of destroying the cockpit area, but the rear fuselage remained largely intact and here, to the delight of investigating RAF officers, was found an intact specimen of the computer associated with the BZA dive-bombing apparatus. Examination of the wreckage also revealed 14 20mm strikes in the fuselage, wings and port engine. A few 0.303in light AA machine gun hits were also found. The aircraft's markings were readily discernible (4D+CT, with the 'C' in yellow and the remainder in black), with a roughly painted letter 'C' in black beneath the swastika on the fin, and from these the aircraft's unit was

Above:
Oberleutnant Hollinde describes how he 'attacked Filton' on 7 March 1941. *J. C. Verryckeh*

immediately estabished. At the subsequent interrogation of the crew their unit was further confirmed to the RAF's knowledgeable POW Interrogation Centre by an examination of the German airman's identity discs — all bore the number 57305, known by British Air Intelligence to have been allocated to III/KG30 at the time of its recent merger with III/KG4.

And so, for the second time in his wartime career, Friedrich Rinck found himself a prisoner of war. The first time had been in the early days of the Dutch campaign — on that occasion he had spent five days in an Amsterdam gaol before the advancing German Army had secured his freedom, but from his new internment there was to be no release until the end of the war.

What happened to the second aircraft, piloted by Leutnant Dahlmann, is not known. It took off shortly before the 4D+CT but apparently failed to find the target.

Despite the mixed results which they achieved, the German Air Force continued to fly pirate-type operations against British targets until late 1942 although, from the invasion of Russia in June 1941 and the associated transfer eastwards of the major part of its bomber force, they were on a decreasing scale. Gradually, however, they became even more hazardous for participating crews as the light AA defences of likely targets were strengthened. The biggest deterrent of all though came when it was decided to use AI radar-equipped night fighters during daylight hours in bad weather. In the main these interceptions were carried out by Beaufighters which, in effect, became the world's first so-called all-weather fighters; initially vectored towards the incoming raiders by fighter controllers using ground-controlled interception radar, they were subsequently able to complete the interception using their own onboard airborne interception radar until, at very close range, visual contact was made. When this occurred, few intruders could expect to escape the devastating fire power of the Beaufighter with its four 20mm cannon and six 0.303in machine guns. As had been the case by night, the new British fighter gradually tipped the scales in favour of the defenders.

Balloon Magic

Peter R. March

More than two centuries ago Europe's first hot-air balloonists demonstrated their ability to get airborne beneath their fragile paper envelopes. The very first successful ascent was made by Pilatre de Rozier and the Marquis d'Arlandres in November 1783, flying just over five miles across Paris. The 122ft circumference balloon was designed and built by two paper-making brothers, the Montgolfiers. In Britain the first brief flight was made by Scotsman James Tytler on 25 August 1784, using a crude fabric bag with hot air provided by a wood burning stove on a platform below. More successful was a young Italian diplomat Vincent Lunardi who made the first 'cross-country' voyage on 15 September 1784 from the

Below:
The Bristol Belle, the UK's first modern hot-air balloon on an early tethered flight in 1967. *Tom Sage*

Below centre:
Cameron's replica of the Montgolfier balloon flying from Bristol in May 1983.

Below right:
Don Cameron sorting out a minor problem on one of his balloons being readied for a test flight in early 1985. *Andrew March*

Honourable Artillery Company grounds in London to Ware in Hertfordshire. Upset by the success of a 'foreigner' managing to make such an impressivve journey by air, James Sadler, a shopkeeper in Oxford, made his version of the Montgolfier balloon and on 4 October 1784 ascended to 200ft near the town, thus becoming the first Englishman to have flown from and returned safely to earth. Subsequently Sadler constructed a gas balloon which he flew in December the same year, following the trend which continued towards this simpler and more effective means of getting aloft. And so it was to be for nearly 180 years.

The art of hot air ballooning did not re-emerge until the early 1960s when Don Piccard was commissioned by the United States Navy to investigate the possibilities of using these craft for military purposes. Although this application did not develop Americans saw the potential for a new sport — hot air ballooning.It was not long before news of this was being picked up on this side of the Atlantic. One of the flying enthusiasts who discussed the development on a summer's evening in 1968 at the bar of the Bristol Gliding Glub was young,

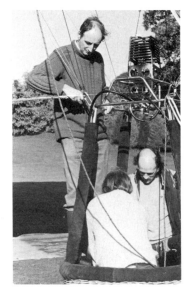

Scots aero engineer Don Cameron. Recalling this recently Don said, 'We thought the idea of hot air ballooning was an interesting one, but we discovered that there wasn't anyone in Europe manufacturing such a thing'. So they did the logical thing and set about designing and constructing one themselves.

The UK's first successful hot-air balloon, the *Bristol Belle* was assembled by Malcolm Brighton at Blackbushe, with manufacture of the envelope contracted to Vacuum Reflex Ltd. Completed in the summer of 1967, the 65,000cu ft, 28-gore free balloon G-AVTL, was flown for the first time from Weston-on-the-

Green, Oxon by Wg Cdr Gerry Turnball on 9 July. (Gore=shaped section of balloon envelope.) Accompanied by Don Cameron, he made a number of short hops on the airfield and when happy with the way it handled he flew it the six miles east to RAF Bicester. Thus a new sport and industry was born in this country, which has

Below left:
The start of the special shaped balloons — *Golly III* for Robertson's Jams.

Below:
These Cameron special shapes have ranged from bottles like *Robinsons Barley Water* G-BKES . . .

since grown to a scale which would have seemed quite inconceivable 20 years ago.

In the following year Messrs Cameron, Turnball, Goldsmith and Westwood formed Omega Aerostatics to manufacture hot-air balloons, based at the premises of RFD-GQ Ltd at Woking, Surrey. Don Cameron was fast approaching an important crossroads in his career. Born in 1940 he was brought up in Scotland, became bitten by the flying bug zooming around in Chipmunks with the Glasgow University Air Squadron before graduating in aeronautical engineering in 1961 and industrial engineering from Cornell, USA in 1963. He joined the British Aircraft Corporation at Filton on return from the USA, moving on to RTZ in Bristol a few years later. But he was becoming increasingly torn between his professional career and his passion for ballooning. Seeking the advice of an old friend and veteran flier from World War 1 he was told; 'If work starts interfering with whisky drinking, give up work'. He took the advice and decided to give up work, not to drink whisky but to take up a full-time commitment to the manufacture of hot air balloons. Breaking away from Omega Aerostatics early in 1970 he set up Cameron Balloons with his wife and another former member of the Bristol Belle Group, photographer and journalist Tom Sage. Production was initially in the basement of No 1 Cotham Park, Bristol before moving in 1972 to a nearby disused church hall, where there was some 7,000sq ft of available space.

In 1970, the first year of production, Cameron Balloons constructed just six examples ranging in size from 56 to 84,000cu ft, of which half were sold abroad. By the end of the 70s more than 100 balloons were being assembled each year,

Above left:
Yellow and black peanuts G-PNUT and G-NUTS . . .

Above:
A pipe for Erinmore pipes . . .

Below:
Cottages like this example exported to Canada . . .

Right:
Balloons at Ashton Park, September 1979.

Above:
A giant hare OH-JBT the symbol of the European Athletic Championships in 1983 . . .

Above right:
Culminating in Malcolm Forbe's replica of his Chateau Balleroi.

75% being exported, with the 1,000th being delivered in 1984. By this time he had outgrown his Cotham factory and had moved to one of the former Wills tobacco factories at Bedminster, Bristol where another aeronautical engineer and balloon enthusiast, Ian Kerr, is now production director with a staff of more than 30 people.

Don Cameron's huge success in rapidly becoming the world's second largest balloon manufacturer is due in no small part to his pioneering use of balloons for aerial advertising and the development of 'special shapes'. After constructing a conventional balloon, for locally based Robertson's Jams, from black nylon decorated in red and white to resemble the company's golly face trademark, he went on a further stage adding a body and arms to produce *Golly III*, a giant balloon gollywog. Since then he has produced more and more exotic shapes including a miscellany of bottles, lorries, cottages, jeans, peanuts and for American millionaire Malcolm Forbes a hot air balloon replica of his chateau in France, a sphinx and an elephant. The clock was turned full circle in 1983 when he was asked by a Belgian customer to construct a flying replica of the original

Montgolfier balloon. Needless to say this was delivered in good time to fly at the 200th anniversary celebrations in Paris.

Don Cameron has always been involved in developments at the frontiers of balloon design and technology many of which have been used for record-breaking and special flights. Included amongst these was the solar balloon designed by Dominic Michaelis. Cameron developed new heat sealing techniques for the 140,000cu ft transparent mylar outer balloon. The double-skinned design trapped and retained heat from the sun on the 'greenhouse' principle. On 25 January 1974 Julian Nott achieved the world altitude record for hot-air balloons (45,836ft) flying Cameron A-375 G-BBGN *Daffodil II* in India. In the same year the Heinken Beer Co commissioned Cameron to build the world's largest (500,000cu ft) hot air balloon. The envelope took over 4,000sq yd of nylon and the load tapes were the size of automobile seat belts. The basket was a replica of Nadar's famous *Le Geant* of 1863, consisting of two floors, door, windows and a locker for the Heinken, all woven in cane (as are all of the baskets for Cameron balloons) by the National Workshops for the Blind in Bristol. The *Gerald A. Heineken* was flown over Snowdon by Tom Sage and captured the world endurance record on 21 November 1975, with a flight of 18hr 56min. It could carry up to 30 people.

In 1973 Cameron Balloons was awarded the silver medal of the Royal Aero Club and the achievement award of the American Lighter-

Above left:
The world's largest hot-air balloon, the Cameron A-530 *Big Bulle* was manufactured in 1981 for a French customer.

Above centre:
The American purchaser of the Cameron 'Hamburger' paid £17,000 for this 'Whopper' in July 1984.
Paul Gingell

Above right:
Many record attempts have been made using Cameron balloons, including this lift of a hang-glider to make a drop from a record height.

Than-Air Society for the successful development of the first hot-air airship. Several production 96,000cu ft non-rigid airships were delivered. Lift was provided by a conventional burner and forward drive came from a propane powered Volkswagen engine; the fins were air-inflated by the propeller's slipstream. Carrying two people it was capable of achieving speeds up to 15kt in still air conditions.

It has not only been as a manufactuer of balloons that Don Cameron has received international recognition, but also as one of the world's leading pilots. In 1972 he crossed the Sahara and the Swiss Alps by hot air balloon for the first time and was involved in the duration record in 1975. But it was not until 1978 that he first became a household name when he attempted, albeit unsuccessfully, to make the first trans-Atlantic crossing. The eyes of the nation watched helplessly as he and his co-pilot Christopher Davey rose and fell in their bid to reach the coast of Spain before their fuel finally gave out.

What is the magic of hot-air ballooning that has led so many people in such a short time to take up this relatively expensive sport? Perhaps it is best explained in Don Cameron's own words:

'Ballooning is a dream, and a reality. It is man's dream of flight, the ability to float above the clouds or a few feet above the trees, or to look at the world as at a map. It has a touch of magic and a feeling of adventure — it is the most

perfect way to fly. The flight of a hot air balloon is entirely different from any other type of aircraft. By turning the burner on and off the pilot can control altitude with precision. These craft can fly to over 20,000ft and yet can hover at a height of 6ft while the pilot talks to passers by. Horizontally the balloon travels with the wind, and steering can only be achieved to a limited extent by searching for varying winds at different altitudes.

'The flight begins with the basket on its side and the envelope spread out down-wind. After the pre-flight checks, a little cold air is put into the envelope. The base of the balloon is held up to form a wide opening and the burner is briefly ignited, sending bubbles of warm air into the balloon. Successive bursts of flame cause the balloon to fill slowly and rise to a vertical position. This process takes about five minutes. As the envelope sways above the basket, the passengers step in and continued heating builds up the lift of the balloon. Maps, instruments

(and refreshments) are placed in the basket and a few more bursts of flame are enough to make the balloon lift gently off. A new adventure has begun!

'Once airborne, the pilot must control altitude by carefully judged use of the burner. With practice, altitude can be controlled completely. A vent can be used to supplement the natural cooling of the balloon, but is normally not used in order to conserve fuel. It is possible to learn this in-flight control tolerably well in just a few hours, although piloting experience and skill go on increasing after hundreds of flights.

'For landing, a field must be chosen in the direction of drift because the balloon cannot be steered left or right. On a windy day, the approach will be controlled by use of the burner and vent, with the object of placing the basket gently on the ground as soon after the 'near' hedge as possible. The basket will turn on its side, and will tend to skid along for a few seconds until the envelope, with the rip panel open, deflates and settles on the ground. On a quiet day, the landing is a completely different operation; it is possible to settle with the envelope inflated above the basket, and to take on fresh pasengers and fuel cylinders before lifting off for another flight.'

Above:
A D-96 Hot-air airship flying round the giant pair of Cameron Jeans on a winter's day at Marsh Benham.

Below:
Cameron DG-19 gas airship at Wroughton in June 1983. The car has a single engine driving two ducted propulsors. *Paul Gingell*

Left:
Ballooning is a dream . . . it has a touch of magic and a feeling of adventure.

Spot that Boeing

gallery 1

Visit any of the world's major international airports outside the USSR and you will be sure to see a Boeing-built airliner. For 30 years this leading US aerospace company has dominated the civil jet airliner market, and looks set to do so for the remainder of this century. The Boeing family started with the 707 first flown on 15 July 1954 and has progressed through the 720, 727, 737, 747, 757 and 767. The following aide memoire will help you to 'spot that Boeing'.

Boeing 707/720

Type: Four-turbofan medium/long range transport, first aircraft flown on 15 July 1954 (Boeing 707/80).

Production: 967 Boeing 707 of which the main variants were the −320B and −320C (482 built); 153 Boeing 720 built. Nearly 300 707/720 remain in airline service.

Recent/current service with: Air France, Air Portugal, Air Zimbabwe, American Trans Air, Arrow Airways, British Caledonian, British Midland, CAAC, Cathay Pacific, Global, Iran Air, Kuwait Airways, Middle East Airlines, Nigeria Airways, Olympic, Saudia, Tarom, Zambia Airways and many others.

Recognition: Underwing mounted engines in four separate pods. Swept narrow chord wing, low set. Circular, narrow body fuselage with the tailplane mounted either side of the tail cone.

Tall, narrow fin and rudder, slightly swept and a small ventral fin.

Variants: The various models of the 707/720 differ mainly in fuselage length and power-plants. The original production 707-120 had a span of 130ft 10in (39.88m) and a length of 144ft 6in (44.04m); the 120B was re-engined with turbofans; the 707-320 was larger with a span of 142ft 5in (43.41m) and length of 152ft 11in (46.61m); the turbo-fan engined −320B had a span of 145ft 9in (44.42m) with the 152ft 11in (46.61m) fuselage, while the −320C was similar but featured a large, port-side forward fuselage freight door. The 720 had the original short-span wings and a shorter fuselage of 136ft 2in (41.50m); the 720B was a turbofan engined variant.

Below left:
Boeing 707-321C of the Rumanian airline Tarom at Bournemouth in August 1984.

Bottom left:
Airline of Egypt's Boeing 707-328C SU-DAB landing at Heathrow. *Andrew March*

Below:
Turkish Airlines Boeing 727-2F2 TC-JBJ on approach. *Daniel March*

Bottom:
Touch down at Bristol Airport for Air Portugal's 727-82QC CS-TBQ. *Andrew March*

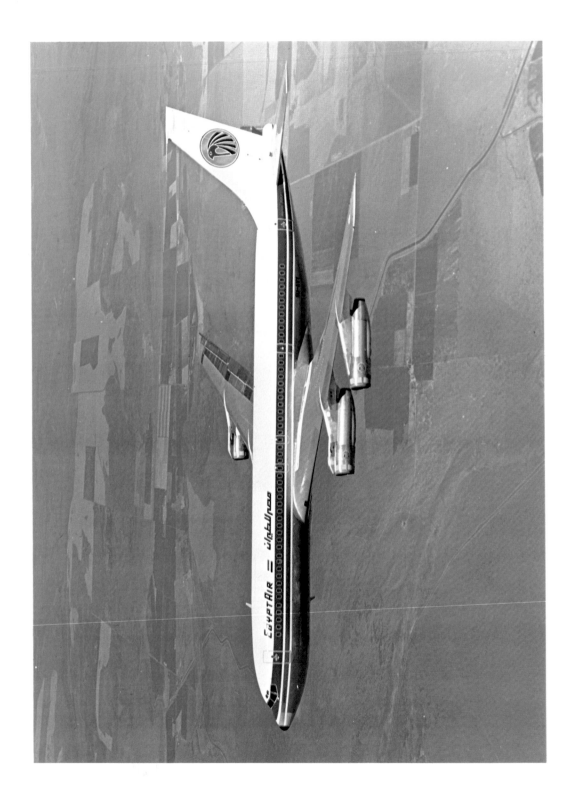

Above:
The turbofan engined Boeing 707-320C, a passenger/cargo variant in the colours of Egyptair. *Boeing*

This picture:
TWA Boeing 727 N54341 flying over snow-capped mountains in the north-west US. *Boeing*

Boeing 727

Type: Three-turbofan medium range airliner, first flown on 9 February 1963.

Production: A total of 1,832 built including 407 series 100, 164 with large freight doors and 1,249 series 200s and Advanced 200s.

Recent/current service with: Many airlines worldwide including: Air Canada, Air France, Alitalia, American Airlines, Ansett, Continental, Dan Air, Delta, Eastern, Federal Express, Iberia, Libyan Arab, Lufthansa, Mexicana, Northwest, Pan American, TAA, Tunis Air, United, Varig and Western Airlines.

Recognition: Three rear-mounted engines, one on top of the fuselage at the base and forward of the fin, the other two in line either side of the rear fuselage. Low set swept wings mid-way along the circular narrow-body fuselage. Swept fin and rudder with T-tailplane on top of the fin.

Variants: The original 407 series 100 aircraft were 10ft (3.05m) shorter than the series 200 which was first flown on 27 July 1967 with more powerful engines and other improvements. A freight variant with a large cargo door (C) and quick-change variant (QC) with the large door and palletised passenger seats has also been built. The Advanced 200 has further powerplant and internal refinements.

Boeing 737

Type: Twin-turbofan, medium range airliner, first flown on 9 April 1967.

Production: Over 1,250 built/ordered by 1985 including 30 series 100, the remainder being series 200 and from 1984 the series 300.

Recent/current service with: 110 airlines worldwide including: Aer Lingus, Air Europe, Air Florida, Air France, All Nippon, Braathens, Britannia Airways, British Airways, CP Air,

Above:
One of Britainnia Airways' early Boeing 737s makes a smokey take-off.

Below:
The distinctive engine nacelles of the Boeing 737-300, the latest production variant, can clearly be seen.

Below centre:
Boeing 747-146 N133TW on finals at Heathrow.

Bottom:
Iran Air's Boeing 747SP-86 EP-IAC shows its short fuselage when compared with the standard version above.

Frontier, India Airlines, Lufthansa, Monarch, Orion, Pacific Western, People Express, Piedmont, Sabena, Saudia, South African Airways, Southwest Airlines, United Airlines, Varig, Vasp, Western, Wien Air.

Recognition: Engines mounted directly under the swept wings. Tubby, circular fuselage with the wings set in the lower section. Tall, angular, slightly swept fin and rudder with the swept tailplane set on the rear fuselage at the base of the rudder.

Variants: Series 100 had a 6ft (1.83m) shorter fuselage, but only 30 built before the larger series 200 entered production. The −200C has a large freight door on the port side of the forward fuselage. Series 300 which entered production in 1984 has a longer fuselage [108ft 8in (33.12m)], slightly increased span wings [94ft 10in (28.91m)], an extended dorsal fin, new engine nacelles projecting forward of the wing and other minor changes.

Boeing 747

Type: Four-turbofan long-range 'Jumbo-jet' airliner, first flown on 9 February 1969.

Production: Over 600 built by 1985 with a further 50 ordered. Current service with many of the world's major airlines including: Air Canada, Air France, Air India. All Nippon, American Airlines, Alitalia, British Airways, Flying Tiger, Iran Air, Japan Airlines, Korean Airlines, Pan American, Qantas, Singapore Airlines, Swissair, TWA, United and World.

Recognition: Underwing mounted engines in four separate nacelles. Swept, low-set wing which narrows towards the tips. Oval, wide body fuselage with a distinctive raised fuselage forward of the wing, incorporating the cabin and flight deck. Tall, swept fin with a fuselage mounted tailplane below the rudder.

Variants: There are 10 main variants of the 747, varying with the different powerplants installed, cabin configuration and weight specifications of the purchasing airlines. Most are hard to distinguish externally. Those most recogniseable are the 747 Combi, 747F, 747SP and the 747-300 (stretched upper deck). The Boeing 747 Combi is a standard size 747 fitted with a large, port-side freight door. The 747F is fitted with an upward hinging nose for freight loading. This special, all-cargo version does not have cabin windows. There are some 747 Combis fitted with the 'F' hinging nose. The 747SP has a 48ft (14.63m) shorter fuselage with a taller fin and rudder and new wing flaps. The raised forward fuselage remains giving a short 'dumpy' look to the aircraft. This 'special performance' version is operated by Pan Am, TWA, Qantas, Iran Air, South African Airways and other airlines. The latest variant is the 747-300 with a stretched upper deck, some 23ft 4in (7.11m) longer than the standard 747. The first operator of the −300 was Swissair.

Boeing 757

Type: Twin-turbofan medium range airliner, first flown on 19 February 1982.

Below:
Swissair was the first customer for the stretched upper deck variant of the 747. *Boeing*

Below centre:
British Airways successfully introduced the Boeing 757 in 1983.

Bottom:
The long fuselage on large engine nacelles can be clearly seen in this landing shot of Monarch's Boeing 757.

Production: Over 140 ordered by 1985.

Recent/current service with: Air Europe, British Airways, Delta, Eastern Airlines, Monarch, LACSA and Singapore AL.

Recognition: Engines in nacelles under the wings. A very long, circular, narrow-body fuselage with swept, low-set wings at the mid-way point. A pronounced lower fuselage bulge for the undercarriage fairing. A tall, swept fin and rudder with a swept tailplane on either side of the rear fuselage below the fin.

Variants: The only variation is in powerplant at present.

Boeing 767

Type: Twin-turbofan medium range airliner, first flown on 8 September 1981.

Production: Nearly 200 ordered by 1985.

Recent/current service with: American Airlines, Air Canada, Britannia AW, Delta, El Al, Kuwait AW, Transbrasil, United Airlines.

Recognition: Turbofans mounted under the swept wings. Circular fuselage with the wings set in the lower section, mid-way between the nose and tail. Very tall swept fin with the tailplane set on the rear fuselage at the base of the rudder.

Variants: Only current differences in powerplant. Stretched 767-300 projected.

Top:
Britannia Airways was the first UK customer for the Boeing 767, taking delivery of the first pair in 1984.

Above:
Trans Brasil was another early operator of Boeing 767s.

Below:
Boeing 747SP operated by China Airlines since April 1980. *Boeing*

Right:
The first Boeing 767 N767BA during its roll-out ceremony at Everett, Wa. *Boeing*

Hunter One
gallery 2

The Hunter One Collection is unique today as the only privately owned and operated collection of vintage British military jet aircraft in the world. Currently consisting of two Hunters, two Sea Hawks, two Meteors, two Vampires, and two Jet Provosts, it was formed in 1981 by Michael Carlton as a living museum of the air.

A London businessman and aviation enthusiast with more than 7,000 hours of flying experience on a wide-range of aircraft types, including gliders, Michael Carlton has a current rating on the Hawker Hunter, flies all the collection aircraft, has held a World Gliding Record and still holds nine British National Records. He is also a member of the Historic Aircraft Association and founder Trustee of the British Light Aviation and Gliding Association.

The story of the collection began with the purchase of the flagship, Hunter 51 G-HUNT, in 1981 and has since seen the addition of Hunter T53 G-BOOM in 1982; Sea Hawks FB5 G-SEAH and FGA6 G-JETH, Meteor T7 G-JETM, Jet Provost T-52s G-PROV and G-JETP in 1983; and two Vampire TIIs, G-VAMP and XD599, and Meteor NF11 G-LOSM in 1984. Currently Hunter G-HUNT,

Meteor NF11 G-LOSM and Jet Provosts G-PROV and G-JETP are appearing at airshows throughout Europe. It is hoped that they will be joined by the Sea Hawks and the Meteor T7 in 1986-7, all of which are at various stages of restoration. Hunter G-BOOM has been operated by an associated company in the United States since April 1985.

The aim of the collection is to present to the public at air displays beautifully refurbished flying examples of some of the most famous names in British jet aviation design and which are all part of the national heritage. The task of restoring, operating and maintaining such a collection of aircraft is monumental, requiring the expert technical knowledge and resources of a full-time engineering staff led by Eric Hayward, demanding and skilled flying by pilots Adrian Gjertsen, Geoff Roberts and Brian Henwood, and the enthusiastic leadership of one man — Michael Carlton.

The senior display pilot and Team Manager

Below:
Michael Carlton in the cockpit of his Hunter F51 G-HUNT.

Right:
The two Hunters, F51 G-HUNT and T53 G-BOOM, over the Dorset coast in 1983. *Arthur Gibson*

Below right:
Meteor NF11 WM167/G-LOSM was added to the display fleet in July 1984.

Adrian Gjertsen is a university graduate and ex-RAF QFI on the Gnat and Hunter with over 1,000 hours on Hunters. Now an airline pilot with Britannia Airways flying Boeing 737s he has been display pilot on G-HUNT since 1980. A member of the Historic Aircraft Association and the collection's chief pilot and approved type rating examiner, Adrian handles all training and standardisation for the team, and as manager deals with all bookings and enquiries for the aircraft.

Display pilot Geoff Roberts is an A2 QFI on the Jet Provost and past member of the 'Poachers' aerobatic team. Now squadron flying instructor on the Tornado with No 9 Squadron at RAF Honington, Geoff has had flying tours on the Phantom in Germany and on Hunters and Hawks at Brawdy as a weapons and tactics instructor. Tornado display pilot for No 9

Squadron in 1983, he joined the Hunter One team that year.

The Historic Aircraft Division of Brencham Ltd was formed in 1981, to manage the Hunter One Collection and the ensuing years have seen a sizeable expansion of the organisation. An administrative head office incorporating a corporate executive aircraft division has been established at Biggin Hill Airport. An operational and engineering base has been set up at Bournemouth-Hurn Airport with the acquisition of Glos Air Ltd, to provide hangarage, crew rooms and an operations centre, plus the addition of a helicopter division and numerous other organisations within the Brencham Group to make continued success of the Hunter One Collection possible.

In addition to purely display flying, the Collection has also been involved with various

Left:
It is hoped that restoration of the first of this pair of Sea Hawks will be completed in 1986.

Below:
This Meteor T7 VZ638-G-JETM was acquired from the Historic Aircraft Museum at Southend in 1983.
Daniel March

Bottom:
Another long-term restoration project is Vampire T11 XK623/G-VAMP.

Above:
The classic lines of the Hunter F51 G-HUNT are well displayed in this Arthur Gibson photograph.
Image in Industry

Below:
Adrian Gjertsen bringing G-HUNT in to land at the team's base at Bournemouth-Hurn Airport.   *PRM*

other air events of public interest in which the aircraft and team members have appeared nationally both in the press, and on radio and television. Notable were the commemoration of the 30th anniversary of the 1953 World Speed Record attained in a Hunter, in which, 30 years on to the day, Neville Duke once again flew his original record course at the controls of Hunter G-BOOM, and the London-Paris Air Race in which a new record of under 40min was established, between the television studios in Paris and London, using the same aircraft.

The past has seen a sad lack of foresight in maintaining our jet aviation heritage and the Hunter One Collection has hopefully taken a step towards redressing the balance of what would otherwise be irretrievably lost.

Above left:
A year long rebuild of the ex-Singapore Jet Provost T52 G-PROV was completed at the end of 1984.

Above:
The Hunter One team for the 1985 display season (left to right) Eric Heyward, Chief engineer; Geoff Roberts, Hunter pilot; Mike Carlton, founder, financier and pilot; Adrian Gjertsen, Chief pilot; Brian Henwood, Meteor pilot.

Below:
The Hunter and Jet Provost en route to an air show in 1985.

Remember the V-Bombers?

gallery 3

Thirty years ago the Royal Air Force was building up its nuclear deterrent force with a trio of four-jet bombers, the Vickers Valiant, Avro Vulcan and Handley Page Victor. The Vulcan served for more than 25 years and was brought back from the brink of retirement to make dramatic raids, using conventional bombs, on the Argentine-occupied Falklands in 1982. The Victor, long retired from its offensive role, remains in service as an air-to-air refuelling tanker, and as such played a key role in the Falklands war. The Valiant, which was relegated to a tanker role much earlier, suffered from airframe fatigue problems and was withdrawn from service more than 20 years ago.

Vickers 706 Valiant

The first of the trio of V-bombers to enter service with the RAF, the Valiant was designed to Specification B9/48 and the Rolls-Royce

Avon-powered prototype WB210 was first flown on 18 May 1951. After some initial development problems the first unit, No 138 Squadron, was formed at RAF Gaydon in January 1955 and the new jet went on to replace the remaining Lincolns and Washingtons with Bomber Command. Of the 104 Valiants produced for the RAF up to August 1957, 11 were reconnaissance B(PR)1s and 14 were multi-role reconnaissance/tankers as B(PR)K1s. Eventually nearly half of the Valiants had the tanker facility. After service with 10 squadrons and action over Egypt during the Suez landings in 1956, all Valiants were withdrawn in 1964 when routine structural testing revealed fatigue problems with the airframe. One complete

Below:
V-bombers over Farnborough in September 1958: Valiant BK1 XD862, Vulcan B1 XA906 and Victor B1 XA936.

51

This picture:
A line-up of Vulcan B2s on the operational readiness platform at RAF Finningley. *Martin Horseman*

This picture:
Vulcan B2 XM569 landing on its last flight at Cardiff-Wales Airport where it joined the Wales Aircraft Museum in 1983. *PRM*

Above:
Valiant BK1 of No 90 Squadron.

Right:
Valiant BK1 XD821 with long range tanks in June 1960.

Below right:
In its anti-nuclear white paint scheme the Valiant was a sleek looking bomber. *Vickers*

example, XD818 — the aircraft which dropped Britain's first H-bombs — has been preserved by the RAF Museum.

Avro 698 Vulcan

The world's first delta wing heavy bomber, the prototype Vulcan VX770 was first flown on 30 August 1952 powered by four Rolls-Royce Avon engines. The second, Bristol Olympus powered prototype VX777 was airborne on 3 September 1953. A total of 45 Vulcan B1s was produced for the RAF between 1955 and 1959. After entering service with No 230 OCU in February 1957 the bomber became operational with No 83 Squadron on 11 July 1957. Most of the B1s were modified to B1A standard with improved engines and electronic counter-measures before retirement in the mid-1960s.

An aerodynamic prototype of the Vulcan B2, VX777 was flown on 31 August 1957 with a modified wing of 12ft greater span. The first production B2, XH533 with up-rated Olympus 200-series engines, followed a year later and XH534 with the extended, bulged tail cone in 1959. Delivery of the Vulcan B2 commenced on 1 July 1960 when No 83 Squadron received XH558 and during the following years also equipped Nos 9, 12, 27, 35 and 617 Squadrons. When the nuclear deterrent role was transferred to the Royal Navy with its Polaris submarines, the Vulcan B2s were reassigned to the low-level strike role and as such equipped Nos 9, 35, 44, 50, 101 and 617 Squadrons until 1981/2. A small number of Vulcans were converted to the strategic reconnaissance role in 1973 and, designated SR2, equipped No 27 Squadron from 1974 to 1981. As an emergency measure during the Falklands war six Vulcans were converted as in-flight refuelling tanker aircraft, with a single fuselage-mounted hose and drogue. These were used for just over a year by No 50 Squadron to replace the Victors assigned to the South Atlantic. A number of Vulcans

have been preserved by the RAF and other UK air museums.

Handley Page HP80 Victor

The last of the three V-bombers to fly, the Victor featured a crescent wing shape and a

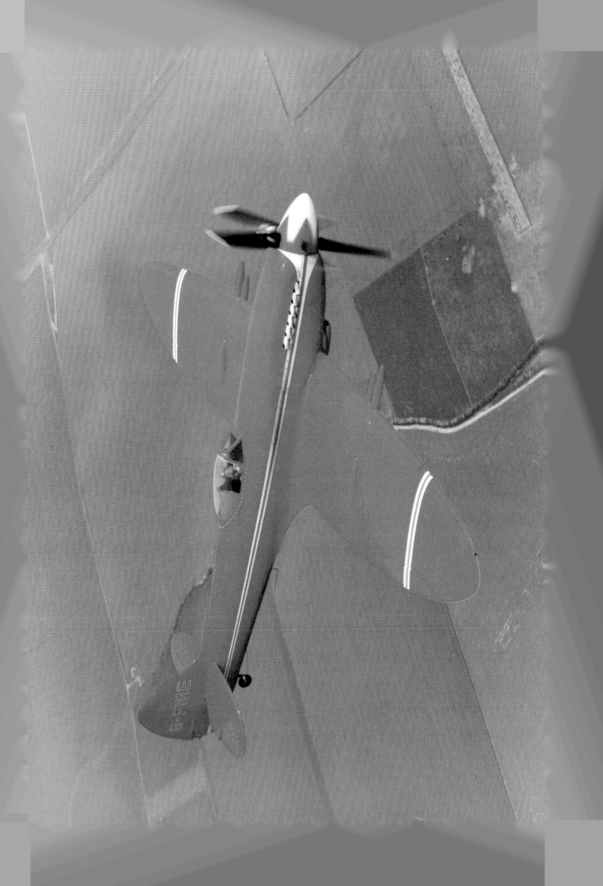

Above:
The Victor's crescent-shaped wing and tailplane can be seen clearly . . .

Top right:
. . . in these two views of XL164.

Above right:
XM717 was the penultimate Victor B2 and was subsequently converted as a tanker . . .

Below:
. . . shown here refuelling a pair of Lightning F6s from No 5 Squadron.

Bottom:
Victor K2s remain in service today — like XH673 shown here in the hemp colour scheme and markings of No 57 Squadron. *Daniel March*

fintip mounted tailplane. The AS Sapphire engined prototype WB771 was first flown on Christmas Eve 1952, with a second aircraft following on 11 September 1954. The lengthened, more powerful first production Victor B1 XA917 was airborne on 1 February 1956, with deliveries to No 232 OCU at RAF Gaydon following in November 1957. Four squadrons (Nos 10,15, 55 and 57) were equipped with the B1. Like the Vulcan, most of these early Victors were given up-dated equipment and electronics and were re-designated B1A. After replacement by the improved B2 from 1961, a number of B1As were modified as three-point tankers and operated by Nos 55, 57 and 214 Squadrons from 1965.

The first Victor B2, powered by R-R Conway engines and with a 10ft increase in wing-span, was flown on 20 February 1959. Production deliveries were made to No 139 Squadron at the end of 1961, this unit becoming the first to become operational with the Blue Steel missile in February 1964. Nine Victors were modified for strategic reconnaissance and operated with No 543 Squadron until 1974. Two-dozen Victor B/SR2s were converted to tankers, the prototype making its first flight on 1 March 1972 and the first K2 delivery being made on 8 May 1974. Most of these ex V-bombers remain in service with Nos 55 and 57 Squadrons today.

Mitchell's Immortal Spitfire

gallery 4

The Supermarine Spitfire was designed by R. J. Mitchell following a long line of development which commenced in 1925 and culminated in his success with the S6B racing seaplane which won the Schneider Trophy outright for Britain in 1931. Designed around Rolls-Royce's new PV-12 engine (later named the Merlin) the Type 300 fighter showed the distinctive lines of the Schneider racers in its fuselage but had a new elliptical shaped wing. Built to Air Ministry specification F5/34, the prototype Spitfire K5054 was first flown on 5 March 1936. The first order for 310 production Spitfire Is was placed on 3 June 1936 and exactly two years later the first deliveries were made to the RAF, entering

service with No 19(F) Squadron at Duxford in July 1938. Sadly, the designer, Reginald Mitchell, had died of cancer a year previously aged just 42, not knowing that his last aircraft was to play such a critical part in the defence of Britain over the next five years.

At the outbreak of war nine RAF fighter

Below:
Mk Ia AR213 is kept flying by the Hon Patrick Lindsay at Booker.

Bottom:
The Battle of Britain Memorial Flight's AB910 is a Mk Vb.

squadrons had been fully equipped with Spitfires and a further two had more than half on strength. On 16 October 1939 Spitfires of Nos 602 and 603 Squadrons shot down a pair of Junkers 88s off the coast of Scotland and on 28 October Flg Off Archie McKellar of No 602 Squadron shot down a Heinkel He111, the first Luftwaffe aircraft to be downed over the British Isles. Production of Spitfires increased rapidly at a growing number of factories and by July 1940 nearly 1,000 were on the strength of 19 RAF squadrons, at the start of the Battle of Britain.

Developments of the basic airframe and engine quickly followed, from the team now led by Joseph Smith who had succeeded Mitchell as Supermarine's chief designer. The develop-

ments were to meet specific Fighter Command requirements: Mks I and II were similar fighters, the latter having an improved Merlin engine, three-blade propeller and increased armour protection: Mks V, VIII, IX and XVI were fighters or fighter-bombers powered by the Merlin 45 series (Mk V), Merlin 60 series (Mk VIII and Mk IX) or the Packard Motors-built Merlin 266 (Mk XVI) and fitted with redesigned wings to take more fuel and a 20mm Hispano cannon (E wing) in place of the Browning machine guns (A wing) or the universal (C wing) which could be adapted to any combination of cannon/machine guns. The subsequent E wing fitted to the Mk IX in 1944 had the bigger 0.5mm Brownings. Other improvements included a larger rudder and for the Mk XVI a

Above left:
Spitfire XIX PM631 was given D-Day markings for the 40th anniversary in 1984.

Left:
NH749 is one of a trio of Spitfire XIVs flying in the UK.

Above:
Stephen Grey's clipped wing Mk IX ML417 joined the flying scene in 1984.

tear-drop cockpit canopy with a cut down rear fuselage. When used for low-level (LF) fighter-bomber duties a clipped wing was standard. The Mk VI and VII were high altitude fighters powered by the Merlin 47 (Mk VI) and Merlin 60 series (Mk VII), both with pressurised cockpits, retractable tailwheel and C wing. The Mks IV, X and XI were unarmed photo-reconnaissance versions with the Mk XIII being an armed variant. A total of over 18,300 Merlin-engined Spitfires was built.

In 1943 the RR Griffon-engined Spitfire XII entered service with Nos 41 and 91 Squadrons at Hawkinge. The new powerplant increased the power, speed and rate of climb, particularly at low level. This was applied to good effect in the Mk XIV which was basically a re-engined Mk VIII with a five-blade Rotol propeller and enlarged fin and rudder, 1,055 being built in 1943/4. Other Griffon-engined Spitfires built were the Mks 21, 22 and 24 fighters/fighter bombers and the Mk XIX unarmed photo-reconnaissance aircraft. The PR19 had a top speed of 460mph and a ceiling of 43,000ft.

Spitfires were also developed for the Fleet Air Arm where they were known as Seafires. Initial versions were converted Spitfire VBs and VCs, the latter forming the basis for the production Seafire IICs of which 262 were built. The Seafire III was the first to feature folding wings. Development mirrored that of the Spitfire and Griffon-engined Seafires (Mk XV and XVII) were built by Cunliffe-Owen and Westlands during the war and the Mks 45-47 (RN equivalents of the Spitfire 21/22) followed postwar.

The last of 22,758 Spitfire variants was built in October 1947 at Eastleigh and the famous fighter remained in RAF service with Royal Auxiliary Air Force squadrons until 1951 and a final trio of PR XIXs with the 'weather' flight at Woodvale until 1957. In 10 years of production and development Mitchell's fighter progressed from the Spitfire I with a top speed of 355mph, maximum weight of 5,280lb and rate of climb of 2,500ft/min to the Seafire 47s 451mph, maximum weight of 12,500lb and climb of 4,800ft/min. The vision of that young designer and his team back in the 1920s in responding to the challenge of the Schneider trophy enabled this country to fight off the apparently over-whelming Luftwaffe challenge in the dark days of 1940 and match the best that Germany could produce in the shape of Messerschmitt Bf109s and Focke-Wulf FW190s in the following years.

Today there are over 70 Spitfires remaining in the UK (and a further 20 or so in Europe) of which about 18 are potentially air-worthy, although at present only half that number can be flown. The following list details the preserved UK Spitfires and their locations:

WG 760

Spitfire I

Ia	K9942 (SD-V)	RAF Museum, Hendon
Ia	P9444 (RN-D)	Science Museum, South Kensington
I	R6915	Imperial War Museum, Lambeth
Ia	X4590 (PR-F)	Battle of Britain Museum, Hendon
Ia	AR213 (QG-A)	Hon P. Lindsay, Booker

Spitfire II

IIa	P7350 (SH-D)	RAF Battle of Britain Memorial Flight, Coningsby
IIa	P7540 (DU-W)	Dumfries & Galloway Aviation Museum, Tinwald Downs

Spitfire V

Vb	AB910 (XT-M)	RAF Battle of Britain Memorial Flight, Coningsby
Vc	AR501 (NN-D)	Shuttleworth Collection, Duxford
Vb	BL614 (ZD-F)	Manchester Air & Space Museum
Vb	BM597 (PR-O)	RAF Church Fenton
Vb	EP120 (QV-H)	RAF Wattisham

Spitfire VIII

T8	MT818 (G-M)	G. Miller, Dinas Powis
VIII	MV154	British Aerial Museum, North Weald

Spitfire IX

IX	MH434 (ZD-B)	Ray Hanna, Duxford
T9	MJ627	M. S. & P. K. Bayliss, Kenilworth
IX	MJ730	G. Black, Hastings
IX	MK356 (21-V)	RAF St Athan Historic Aircraft Museum
T9	ML407	E. N. Grace, St Merryn
IX	ML417	B. J. S. Grey, Booker
IX	ML427 (ST-I)	Birmingham Museum of Science
IX	NH238 (D-A)	Warbirds of Great Britain, Bitteswell
T9	PV202	S. W. Atkins, Saffron Walden
IX	TE517	R. Lamplough, Falfield, Glos
IX	TE566	G. Black, Hastings

Spitfire XI

XI	PL983	R. Fraissinet, East Midlands

Spitfire XIV

XIV	MT847	RAF Cosford Aerospace Museum
XIV	MV262 (42-G)	Warbirds of Great Britain, Bitteswell
XIV	MV293	Warbirds of Great Britain, Bitteswell
XIV	MV370 (AV-L)	Whitehall Theatre of War, London
XIV	NH749	Privately owned, Cranfield
XIV	NH799	Warbirds of Great Britain, Bitteswell
XIV	G-FIRE	Classic Air Displays, Elstree
XIV	RM689 (AP-D)	Rolls-Royce, East Midlands
XIV	SM832	Warbirds of Great Britain, Bitteswell

Spitfire XVIe

XVIe	RW382	RAF Uxbridge
XVIe	RW386 (RAK-A)	Warbirds of Great Britain, Bitteswell
XVIe	RW388 (V4-U)	R. J. Mitchell Memorial Hall, Hanley, Staffs
XVIe	RW393 (XT-A)	RAF Turnhouse
XVIe	SL542 (4M-N)	RAF Coltishall
XVIe	SL574	RAF Bentley Prior
XVIe	SL674	RAF Memorial Biggin Hill
XVIe	TB252 (GW-H)	RAF Leuchars
XVIe	TB382	RAF Exhibition Flight, Abingdon
XVIe	TB752 (KH-Z)	RAF Manston Memorial Hall
XVIe	TB863	B. J. S. Grey, Booker
XVIe	TB885	Shoreham APS
XVIe	TD248 (DW-A)	RAF Sealand
XVIe	TE184 (LA-A)	Ulster Folk & Transport Museum, Co Down
XVIe	TE311	RAF Exhibition Flight, Abingdon
XVIe	TE356	RAF Scampton
XVIe	TE392	RAF Credenhill, Hereford
XVIe	TE462	Royal Scottish Museum of Flight, East Fortune
XVIe	TE476	RAF Northolt

Spitfire XVIII

XVIII	HS649	G. Black, Hastings
XVIII	SM969	Warbirds of Great Britain, Bitteswell

Spitfire XIX

XIX	PM631 (DL-E)	RAF Battle of Britain Flight, Coningsby
XIX	PM651	RAF Benson
XIX	PS853	RAF Battle of Britain Memorial Flight, Coningsby
XIX	PS915	RAF Battle of Britain Memorial Flight, BAe Preston

Spitfire F21

F21	LA198 (JX-C)	RAF Locking
F21	LA226	RAF Memorial Biggin Hill
F21	LA255 (LX-V)	RAF Wittering

Spitfire F22

F22	PK624 (RAU-T)	RAF Abingdon
F22	PK664 (V6-B)	RAF Binbrook

Spitfire F24

F24	PK683	R. J. Mitchell Hall, Southampton
F24	PK724	RAF Museum, Hendon

Seafire XVII

XVII	SX137	Fleet Air Arm Museum, RNAS Yeovilton
XVII	SX300	Midland Air Museum, Coventry
XVII	SX336	Privately owned, Newark

Seafire F46

F46	LA564	P. R. Arnold, Newport Pagnell

Silver Jubilee of the 10-year Fighter

Bryan Philpott

In July 1985 the Lightning completed 25 years of squadron service with the Royal Air Force: not bad for an aeroplane that had been forecast to stay in front-line use for 10 years!

The Lightning is the only British-designed and built Mach 2 fighter to serve the RAF, a distinction that it is likely to hold for evermore. But things could have been so different for this superlative weapons system. Conceived by W. E. W. Petter, of Gnat and Canberra fame, and nursed to maturity by Freddie (now Sir Fredrick) Page, the Lightning was indeed lucky to have reached production at all.

In 1954 the Defence White Paper, hinted that a supersonic interceptor of British design,

would fly that year, and duly on 4 August the English Electric P1, in the hands of Wg Cdr Roland Beamont, made its maiden flight from Boscombe Down. Three years later, in fact on the very day the first P1B made its first flight, 4 April 1957, the infamous 1957 White Paper, prophesised no future for manned interceptors, claiming that future defence lay in the hands of surface-to-air missiles. Many projects including Avro's supersonic bomber, the Saunders Roe SR53, the thin-wing Javelin and derivatives of the Hunter, were all cancelled, and the decline of the British Aircraft Industry as a totally independent entity, began.

But by then two P1s and the P1B had flown and were well into their test programmes. Cancellation then would have been very misguided, therefore it was agreed that the project could continue, since it was believed that the aircraft would have a useful 10-year life

Below:
The first English Electric P1 WG760 was first flown in 1954 and is now preserved at RAF Binbrook.
Andrew March

Above:
Second prototype P1 WG763 was used for development flying between 1955 and 1965.

Left:
The only P1B, XA847, photographed at Farnborough in 1957.

as an interceptor in height bands above those that could be reached by Meteor 8s and Hunters then currently forming Fighter Command's first-line of defence.

Although the P1 is often referred to as a Lightning, it was in fact purely a research vehicle and close study of it will reveal that it had very few similarities to the aircraft that was eventually to become so popular with squadron pilots.

In the immediate postwar years, the government called a halt to all experiments in manned supersonic flight, claiming that the risk to life was far too great. Work carried out in this field was limited to unmanned rocket powered projectiles launched mainly from Mosquito aircraft. This 'head-in-the-sand' attitude saw the cancellation of the promising Miles M52 research aircraft, which could have given Britain a lead in supersonic flight. In 1947 when the Americans succeeded in breaking the so called 'sound barrier' with the rocket-powered Bell X-1, attitudes began to change and the Ministry of Supply (MoS) issued Experimental Requirement 103 (ER103), which was for a research aircraft capable of exploring transonic and low supersonic speeds.

English Electric and Fairey Aviation responded with the P1 and FD2 respectively. The latter was purely an experimental aircraft, but the former was built to fighter-strength

factors and had the capability of being developed into a practical fighter.

Petter favoured twin Avons for his shoulder wing design which incorporated 60° sweep and a low set tailplane, but these were not available when required, so he settled for twin Armstrong Siddeley Sapphire ASSa5 engines. By the time design work had been completed, the original MoS design study had been expanded into specification F23/49, which broadened the requirement to include guns, a sighting system and fighter-type handling characteristics. This specification did not go out to general tender, since the work already carried out made it sensible to award English Electric a contract for two prototypes and a structural-test airframe.

Petter's idea to mount the engines one above the other with a staggered layout, reduced the frontal area by 50%, thus giving the P1 a frontal area equal to a single-engined aircraft, but the thrust of two to push it into the transonic region. From the very beginning the designer had favoured a low set tailplane, believing that a 'T' tail would cause unacceptable pitch-up. But pressure from those who did not share this view resulted in the production by Shorts of the SB5 to be used as a test vehicle. This aircraft had variable geometry wings, and a tailplane that could be mounted on top of the fin or below the fuselage. The SB5 flew with a variety of wing sweeps (adjustment only being possible on the ground) and with the tailplane in both positions. Eventually it proved Petter's theory correct and all P1s and Lightnings had the low set tailplane. Cross-wind handling problems with swept wing aircraft caused, in the main, by their high rolling moment and poor effect from swept trailing edge controls, resulted in the aircraft's ailerons being hinged at right angles to the line of flight, another characteristic retained on all models.

Eventually work on the P1 serialled WG760 was completed and in July 1954 it was moved by road to Boscombe Down for its initial flights. It was realised at this time that the available thrust from the twin Sapphires was only capable of pushing the aircraft beyond Mach 1, above this the thrust gave such poor acceleration that the aircraft would run out of fuel before it reached its limiting Mach number. Nonetheless it proved the airframe design potential and handling qualities. A further advantage of the twin layout was that the aircraft could fly on one engine without the associated asymmetric problems, an advantage that would allow it to return to base quite safely on one engine.

Supersonic aircraft do not have the best gliding characteristics, so in the event of failure on a single-engined machine the aircraft was usually lost — as more often than not the pilot would make his descent by courtesy of Martin-Baker. The P1 therefore provided a much appreciated safety factor, for the total recovery of an airframe and pilot was much preferable than just the recovery of the pilot.

The twin engines of the P1 also enabled it to cruise at supersonic speed without the use of reheat, thus saving fuel which would be burned in enormous quantities in the case of a single engined aircraft attempting to do the same. However, fuel consumption was a problem, and gave the P1 — and indeed the early Lightnings — a very short duration. The procurement of 20 pre-production test aircraft did help to over-

Left:
Prototype Lightning T4 XL628 leading XG331, a development F1 in a stream take-off.

Below left:
The last of the pre-production batch of F1s first flown on 1 August 1959, XG337 was later modified to F3 standard for development flying.

Above:
Lightning F1A XM183 of No 226 OCU taking off from RAF Coltishall.

come many problems before the aircraft entered service, but fuel consumption although improved in the F1, was not one that was totally solved by these aircraft.

In July 1955 WG760 was joined by WG763 in the flight test programme, and it was this aircraft that English Electric displayed at the SBAC Display Farnborough that year. This machine was fitted with guns and a 250gal ventral tank and took an active part in development flying until it became an instructional airframe at Henlow in November 1965; it now resides in Manchester's Air and Space Museum.

The provision of three P1B prototypes and 20 pre-production aircraft, enabled work to proceed across a very wide spectrum thus, in theory, reducing the time of entry into squadron service. In practice, however, although the idea was sound and had been adopted successfully in other countries, there were problems in handling such a large number of what were virtually prototype aircraft. Despite the problems created in supplying effective back-up to all airframes, the Lightning did enter service quicker than it would have if all tests had been restricted to just three aircraft, but the time saved was not as great as had originally been anticipated. The first P1B (XA847) was powered by Avons, and reached Mach 1.2 on its maiden flight on 4 April 1957. In October 1958 the aircraft was officially named by the then Chief of the Air Staff, Sir Dermot Boyle, and in November it became the first British built aircraft to fly at twice the speed of sound when it reached Mach 2. This event was commemorated by a plaque on the port side of the aircraft.

By this time five aircraft were flying and English Electric had announced that it was in large scale production for the Royal Air Force. It was this press release that stated that the company estimated it would stay in service for 10 years.

As development flying continued work was also proceeding on the initial order for 50 aircraft which were to be designated F1. The fuel consumption problem was partly met by the addition of a 250gal ventral tank, but was by no means the final answer. Flight refuelling was another obvious means, with a follow-up being a long-range version with increased fuel capacity. The 1957 White Paper had put money into short supply, especially for the develop-

ment of systems for a fighter aircraft, so it is perhaps not surprising that the RAF could only muster lukewarm enthusiasm for spending money on what would possibly be a very short-term investment.

The prototype P1B, XA847, was fitted with a dry-link flight refuelling probe and after successful installation and flight trials, it was introduced on to XM169, which was the first of the second batch of 30 airframes covered by the initial order. This aircraft therefore became the first F1A, of which 30 were scheduled for production but only 28 were built. The ventral tank was also viewed as the most likely part into which the Scorpion rocket motor could be installed. The company had been eyeing this addition for sometime, as a method not only to

Top:
No 92 Squadron was equipped with F2s, like this example XN790 and . . .

Above:
. . . the improved F2A XN772 for service with RAF Germany.

Right:
The Lightning F3 saw service for 20 years from 1964 to 1984; during the final period as a training and display aircraft with the LTF at Binbrook.

boost the Lightning's rate of climb, but also to increase its service ceiling where the rarefied air made the jet engine inefficient and brought the rocket motor into its element. Plans were afoot to install the Double Scorpion into a jettison-able pack aft of the ventral tank, and the installation was tested in a Canberra aircraft which went to 70,310ft in August 1957. However, these plans came to nothing and the Lightning was never able to show its prowess with such an installation.

The ability of the Lightning to climb to 30,000ft from a standing start in 2½min, was no mean feat, and one that is still very commendable some 30 years later. But such a climb to operational altitude, followed by acceleration to interception speed, allowed one pass at a potential target, if sufficient fuel was to remain to enable the aircraft to make a safe recovery within operational limits. The old bogey of fuel consumption was therefore a limiting factor and the Scorpion would not greatly improve this aspect of the aircraft's design envelope despite the fact that it would have enabled it to get to altitude very quickly.

Despite the shortcomings of its range, the Lightning was cleared for issue to the service and the first unit to receive Lightnings was the Central Fighter Establishment then based at Coltishall, in December 1959. Pilots of the Air Fighting Development Squadron of CFE had been flying Lightnings from Warton in 1958, so the aircraft was not new to all of them when it started its service life with the evaluation squadron. Sharing Coltishall with CFE was No 74 Squadron which had been earmarked to be the first operational squadron to receive the aircraft, so its pilots were able to study the Lightning at close quarters whilst they awaited the day they received their own aircraft. This happy occasion occurred on 29 June 1960, when 74's first aircraft was flown by Jimmy Dell to Leconfield, as Coltishall's runway was being repaired.

In early July work on the runway was complete, so the first No 74 Squadron Lightning, F1 XM165, was flown together with four others from Leconfield to Coltishall. The Mach 2 era had arrived at squadron level.

At this time there were no two-seat versions in service, so pilots were familiarised with the aircrafts' systems in a specially equipped two-seat Hunter T7, which often operated as one of a pair with a Lightning during practice interception. The increase in performance that the pilots had to become accustomed to can be appreciated by the fact that the Lightning had to give the Hunter a 28,000ft start before it took off to operate with the earlier fighter.

Another new factor that required major refurbishment was that the Lightning was a completely integrated weapons system. Its radar was closely related to the Firestreak missiles it carried, and although it was equipped with two 30mm Aden cannon, the infra-red homing missiles were its main armament. But the pilots quickly got used to the new aircraft, its weapons, and operational parameters, and soon it was taking part in exercises in which it proved that at last the RAF had a fighter that was on a par with anything else in the western world.

In September 1960 No 74 Squadron was able to provide a four-aircraft aerobatic team for the SBAC display at Farnborough, which speaks volumes not only for the pilots, but also their commanding officer, Sqn Ldr J. F. G. Howe, who moulded them to such an efficient team in such a short time.

The second squadron to equip with the Lightning was No 56 which received its first F1A on 14 December 1960. This unit was to become very much involved in the development of long range flights with the Lightning, and was the first to undertake an overseas deployment using flight refuelling. This took place on 23 July 1962 when two aircraft flew non-stop Akrotiri, Cyprus in 4hr 22min. This was followed by several similar sorties all aimed at proving the effectiveness of the F1A's flight refuelling capability, and laid the foundations of essential training to ensure that deployments to Cyprus, Malta and Singapore became common for the Lightning.

The famous 'Treble One' squadron became the third unit to take delivery of Lightnings, the initial aircraft arriving in April 1961. The squadron had made its name by looping 22 Hunters at the 1958 SBAC display, and very much earlier when Sqn Ldr John Gillan had flown a Hurricane to Edinburgh in record time from Northolt, a record that the squadron held until 1955 when it broke it with a Hunter repeating Gillan's feat at 717mph. But record breaking was not for the Lightning, at least not officially, and No 111, like the other two

Left:
The F6 first entered service with No 5 Squadron in October 1965, remaining with the same squadron today. This pair of No 5's Lightnings is taking on fuel from a Victor K1A of No 55 Squadron.

Below:
The F6 saw service in the Far East with No 74 Squadron, the unit's XR769 shown here at RAF Tengah in 1968, and with . . .

Above:
. . . No 56 Squadron in the Near East; an armed example here landing at RAF Akrotiri, Cyprus.

squadrons, quickly settled down to become proficient with its new interceptor.

The F1A differed from the F1 in radio and internal equipment; the only external difference was the addition of an external duct along the lower fuselage, and a flight refuelling probe beneath the port wing. These two types were followed by the F2, for which an order for 44 was placed, the prototype flying on 11 July 1961 from Samlesbury. The F2 was externally similar to the F1A, retaining the pointed 'witches hat'

fin/rudder and extended cable ducting, the only recognisable difference being the intake duct on top of the spine for the aircraft's DC stand-by generator. Internally there was new TACAN, a liquid oxygen breathing system and for the first time, a fully variable reheat replacing the four-position system used on the F1 and F1A.

Leaving aside the two-seat versions, the next Lightning was the F3 which was referred to by English Electric in 1963 as a 'stretched' version. This aircraft brought radical changes: the familiar pointed fin/rudder was replaced by one with a square top of greater area; the Avon 300 series engines had increased thrust of 13,500lb each boosted to 16,000 by reheat, which was double that available to the original P1A; and another important change was to the weapons system. The Firestreaks were replaced by Red Top missiles, using improved Ferranti A123B Airpass radar. It was the installation of the larger missiles, which had a longer burning time than the Firestreaks, that led to the 15% increase in fin area. The changes to the aircraft's structure enabled a slight increase in internal fuel, but the thirsty Avons negated this as far as increased range was concerned, again flight refuelling equipment was fitted. The F3 was not fitted with any form of cannon armament, and therefore became the first all missile armed fighter to enter RAF squadron service.

The first F3 was delivered to CFE on 1 January 1964, and the first squadron to operate them was No 74 which started to receive its aircraft in April 1964.

The F3 was ordered in greater quantity than any other Lightning, a total of 70 being specified; some of which were later modified to F6. The problem of fuel consumption had been a nagging one right from the very early days, but it was not until 1963 that proposals which had constantly been put forward and rejected, were at last accepted. The Warton design staff developed a greatly increased capacity ventral tank fitted with two fins to maintain directional stability, and this was initially tested on XP697 which also appeared at this time with the new

cambered leading edge. The new wing had been tried as early as 1957 on the P1A, and the tank and ventral fin on P1B XA847 in 1959. The wing had reduced outer-panel sweep and increased leading edge camber, so that lift was improved at high angles of attack and subsonic drag was reduced. There was virtually no drag penalty, but range was increased by about 20% as a result of the increased wing efficiency. On the new wing the ailerons became inset and although there was no increase in span, the area increased by about 13sq ft. The overall effect was not only to increase the Lightning's range, but also its high-altitude performance particularly at subsonic speeds. A further addition at this time was the introduction of overwing ferry tanks, these plus the ventral tank (which was not jettisonable) increased fuel capacity by over 1,000gal.

Despite what has been published to the contrary, the overwing tanks were never fitted to operational F3 aircraft, although such a machine was used with dummy tanks to test the installation and handling. The confusion has probably arisen because these changes were introduced to the latter half of the F3 contract when the aircraft were initially designated F3A or F3ER/6/Int, but this was soon abandoned in favour of the designation F6 for RAF service aircraft. The first F6, which had originally been the fifth production F3, made its maiden flight on 17 April 1964 and was then used on development flying during which it was fitted with a new weapons pack carrying 2in rocket projectiles. The first production F6s were from a batch of 16 F3s and were basically interim models lacking the strongpoints for the overwing tanks. Later 15 of these aircraft were withdrawn from service as full specification F6s became available, and they were modified to the full standard before once again being taken on squadron strength. The first squadron to receive the F6 was No 5, which gave up its Javelins in October 1965 and received its first F6 on 10 December, although prior to this it had been operating a T5 and Hunters equipped with F3/F6 OR946 instrumentation. It is interesting to note that this unit is still operating the Lightning 20 years later; together with No 11 Squadron; these are the last two operational Lightning squadrons in the RAF.

The final single-seat version to enter squadron service was the F2A, this being considered by many Lightning pilots to be the best of all

marks. This aircraft was basically an F2 brought up to F6 standard by the addition of the large ventral tank and cambered wing, although the latter was not stressed to take the overwing tanks. The original nose-mounted twin 30mm Adens were retained, but with the revised gun pack in the forward part of the ventral tank, the aircraft could be fitted with additional cannons. Of the original 44 F2s manufactured, 32 were converted to F2A configuration and served mainly with Nos 19 and 92 Squadrons in Germany. Soon after these squadrons started to receive F2As, rumours started that the Lightning was to be replaced by the McDonnell Douglas F4 Phantom. This eventually proved to be the case, and gradually the Lightning was phased out.

The only Lightnings not so far mentioned have been the two-seat versions. The T4 was basically a two-seat version of the F1A and the T5 a similar conversion of the F3, with the small ventral tank. Both aircraft saw long service with OCUs and on the squadrons, where they could be used as front-line aircraft since they retained all the equipment of the single-seater from which they were derived.

Versions of the F6 and T5 were exported to Saudi Arabia and Kuwait. The latter trainer was known as the T55 and was equipped with the large F6 type ventral tank. These comparatively small export orders came late in the aircraft's development, but they serve to illustrate what might have been. There is no doubt that if the Lightning had received proper government backing and support, at the time it was needed most, the aircraft stood a real chance of becoming the standard equipment of NATO air forces instead of the F-104, but that is another story.

There can be no doubt that this British-built aircraft has done all that was asked of it, was popular (and still is) with service pilots, and 25 years after its service debut is still fulfilling a vital role in the defence of this country alongside much more sophisticated aircraft, which can still find their work cut-out in a one-to-one situation with a well handed Lightning.

Hopefully there are enough airframes and spares available for the RAF to retain a Lightning in the historic aircraft flight, for it certainly deserves an accolade similar to that given to its illustrious contemporary, the Vulcan, and its forefathers the Spitfire and Lancaster.

BOAC 1939 to 1974
A historic review

In November 1937, following trenchant criticisms in Parliament, a committee of inquiry was appointed under the chairmanship of Lord Cadman. The principal recommendations of its report were that British external air transport should be handled by a small number of well-founded organisations; that British companies should not compete on the same routes; Imperial Airways should concern itself primarily with long distance air services; there should be a close working liaison between Imperial Airways and British Airways.

The Government accepted the principles of the report, but for a number of reasons it decided on a course of nationalisation. A bill was introduced late in 1938 that covered the merging of Imperial Airways with British Airways to form the state-owned British Overseas Airways Corporation. The bill received royal assent in August 1939. The corporation was formally established on 24 November 1939 under the chairmanship of Sir John Reith.

At the outbreak of war in September, civil operations came under the control of the Secretary of State for Air. On the day of appointment, 1 April 1940, BOAC officially acquired Imperial Airways and British Airways, but it was an event washed over and obscured by the tides of war.

During the early days of hostilities Imperial Airways reopened a service to Paris, but the collapse of France in June 1940 and the entry of Italy into the war disrupted most British air communications. A new route joining Britain with the east and south had to be found and opened quickly.

Flying boats were used to carry Government-sponsored personnel through Lisbon to West Africa, there linking with the trans-African route pioneered in 1936. This connected with a new Horseshoe Route — from South Africa to

Below:
Former Imperial Airways AW Ensigns received camouflage and were used for BOAC's international flights from Whitchurch in 1940.
British Airways Collection (courtesy the RAF Museum)

Australia — at Khartoum. This was in fact the usable parts of the original Australian and South African routes, which joined at Cairo. When the route through Malaya and Singapore was cut by Japanese invasion, BOAC, in association with Qantas, ran a 3,512-mile non-stop service between Ceylon and Perth, Western Australia.

But of all BOAC wartime operations the most dangerous was undoubtedly its ball-bearing run to Sweden, and the most significant for its future, the Transatlantic Return Ferry Service. On the first, BOAC, using a variety of unarmed aircraft in civil markings from Whitleys to Mosquitoes, flew 800 miles between Leuchars in Scotland and Stockholm. They carried important allied personnel over hostile territory in both directions and from Sweden brought back all-important sets of ball bearings. More than 1,200 such flights were made.

The Atlantic was a tough route, its weather the most variable in the world. But many of the aircraft built in the US and Canada for the Allies had to be flown to Britain and their crews returned to North America for another collection. An air service was opened in May 1941 using Liberators to return the ferry crews to North America. It was completely taken over by BOAC in September 1941. Thus began the first ever, regular, two-way, all-the-year-round service across the North Atlantic. The experience and accumulated data proved invaluable in the postwar years. The service continued when fighting ceased and on 10 February 1946 the 2,000th crossing was completed.

In May 1941 BOAC bought three long-range Boeing 314 flying boats at a cost of £259,000 each to maintain the vital UK-West Africa link. they were also used to fly a regular two-way Atlantic service. By the end of hostilities BOAC had flown more than 57 million miles, uplifted nearly 50 million pounds of cargo and mail and carried 280,000 passengers. Its fleet numbered 160 aircraft and its route network spanned 54,000 miles.

With the end of the European war, BOAC and its partner Qantas tackled the reorganisation of the longest air route in the world — England to Australia. Starting with a once-weekly service on 31 May 1945, it was increased to twice weekly on 15 July. More than 12,000 miles between Hurn and Sydney were covered in 63 hours, by Lancastrians, making it the fastest as well as the longest route in the world.

Before 1939, flying boats had taken nine days. With a new fleet of Yorks the South African route was reopened in partnership with South African Airways during November 1945. Although Britain was gradually moving over to a civil footing, BOAC still had a number of military commitments to fulfil. At the end of 1945 BOAC's 30 routes exceeded 70,000 miles and about 10,000 passengers were handled each week.

In the autumn of 1945, development flights were started with converted Halifax bombers — renamed Haltons — to West Africa. There were also surveys of the route to South America.

As the bemused and war-battered world of 1945 tried once more to adjust its priorities, airlines were already picking up the threads of peacetime traffic and looking ahead to the future pattern of trade. Even with its extensive background of Imperial Airways' experience and wartime operations, BOAC found forecasting difficult against fast altering patterns of commerce, loyalties and changing aircraft types. Its first responsibility was to those countries that before 1939 had formed the British Empire of Nations. Routes connecting them with Britain were rapidly re-established. Some countries in the enthusiasm of newly found independence wanted to form their own airlines. BOAC helped them with advice and often finance.

Routes similar to those of pre-1939 were put back on a peacetime footing with converted wartime equipment. There was little else. Lancastrians (ex-Lancaster bombers) went to Sydney, Haltons (ex-Halifax bombers) to Cairo and West Africa, Yorks (military transports) to India and South Africa, Hythe flying boats (Sunderland 3s) to Australia. For a short time, until January 1947, the old faithful 'C' class boats continued to plod round the South Africa-India horseshoe. But none of these loyal friends was suitable for the rugged, exacting North Atlantic — the route of the future. For five years Boeing 314 flying boats had given sterling service on the mid-Atlantic UK-US route. But clearly they were no match for the modern, long-range land-planes then becoming available. The Boeings were later sold in 1948.

Britain had no aircraft of a range and capacity that made commercial sense on the North Atlantic. To maintain its international competitive position BOAC ordered five Lockheed Constellation 049s and ran a westbound schedule of 19¾hr on a twice-weekly London-

Above:
BOAC took over this Liberator in September 1941 to operate a North Atlantic service to return ferry crews to North America.
British Airways Collection (courtesy the RAF Museum)

Below:
Three Boeing 314A flying boats were purchased by BOAC in 1941 to operate on West African and Atlantic services.
British Airways Collection (courtesy the RAF Museum)

Right:
BOAC's Speedbird can just be seen on this Mosquito returning to Leuchars from a 'ball-bearing' run to Sweden in 1943.
British Airways Collection (courtesy the RAF Museum)

New York service starting on 1 July 1946. This established the first British commercial air service between London and New York.

But by the turn of the decade, the first of the postwar commercial designs was beginning to replace older equipment. Five ex-Aer Linte (Ireland) Constellation 749s were put on the Australian service in 1948. The Solent, first of the post-war flying boats, took over African routes.

On 23 August 1949 BOAC introduced one of the most successful of all immediate postwar designs — the Argonaut — a well-proven Douglas C-54/DC4 airframe, built in Canada and powered by Rolls-Royce Merlin piston engines. After being delivered several months ahead of schedule, this reliable combination pointed the way to the future by establishing the first BOAC all-landplane service to Tokyo. The days of the flying boat were numbered. Argonauts cut two days off their schedules to the Far East. By the year's end, Boeing Stratocruisers with two-deck comfort were flying between London and New York, calling at Prestwick. Scheduled westbound time at 19¾hr was the same as the Constellation, which went mainly through Shannon.

Following withdrawal of its Tudor aircraft after unexplained failure, BSAA had been left in a difficult and uncompetitive position. The Minister of Civil Aviation decided that for this reason and others, which included overall improvement to flexibility and efficiency, BSAA should be merged with BOAC. Royal assent to the Airways Corporation Bill, which made the amalgamation law, was received on 30 July 1949 and BSAA ceased to exist.

For BOAC the 1950s began filled with bright hope and promise. New aircraft were in prospect that looked like transforming its financial record. In the five years from April 1946 to March 1951, BOAC's accounts had shown losses totalling £32 million. At the turn of the decade the last of the war-associated aircraft types was retired and 1950 saw BOAC with an all-postwar fleet. In March 1950 deliveries of a fleet of 25 Handley Page Hermes began and first services left London for Accra in August. Later in the year these aircraft replaced Solents and Yorks on all African routes. Stratocruisers were popular on the North Atlantic and traffic increased steadily. In August 1950 BOAC earned for the first time in its history £2 million in a month from all its services.

In March 1951 development flying began with a new revolutionary jet transport, the DH

Comet 1, and on 2 May 1952 BOAC made commercial airline history when this, its first jetliner, left London Airport for Johannesburg, inaugurating the world's first pure jet passenger service. By September, the ninth and last of the Comet fleet had been delivered. BOAC was triumphantly ahead of its competitors on the Far East and South African routes and doing well on its other services. It was able to announce an overall surplus, for the first time, in its 1951/52 financial year. It totalled a modest £274,999, but members of BOAC were justifiably proud of this achievement. They felt that it was a small beginning to greater things.

Fleet re-equipment continued at a rapid pace. Comet 1s took over BOACs long eastern route, the 10,400-mile London-Tokyo link, slashing 50hrs off the Argonaut time. Preparations were made to introduce Comet 2s on the South American route and the first production model of this type was flown on 27 August 1953. So well was the new equipment programme proceeding, that BOAC retired its Hermes fleet during October 1953.

But in January 1954 disaster struck suddenly. One of the Comet fleet crashed off Elba in the Mediterranean. Immediately all Comets were withdrawn and an extensive programme of investigation initiated. On 23 March operations were restarted but only 16 days later another Comet crashed near Naples and the aircraft's Certificate of Airworthiness was withdrawn. The rewards of successful innovation are great but the penalties of unsuccessful innovation are

greater. It took BOAC nearly 10 years to overcome this substantial loss of its earning ability. BOAC had great difficulties in maintaining its scheduled operations. It cancelled services to South America in April and by July had resuscitated some of its remaining Hermes aircraft. They went back on the East African route.

BOAC bought other aircraft where it could, including 12 Constellation 749s and seven Stratocruisers, to help its hard-pressed fleet. It was not until more than 18 months later — the end of 1955 — that the first two aircraft of a new Bristol Britannia 102 propeller-turbine fleet were delivered. For a number of manufacturing reasons their delivery had been put back substantially. Britannias took over on a number of BOAC routes, starting with African services and on 19 December 1957, a long-range version, the 312, began the first gas-turbine transatlantic service to New York. Its late delivery also did not help the corporation in its attempts to get back to financial self-sufficiency. Anticipating delays to its Britannia fleet, BOAC had ordered 10 piston-engined Douglas DC-7C aircraft as a stop-gap. These aircraft began operating between London and New York on 6 January 1957 and two months later the route was extended to San Francisco for the first time.

As a result of probably the most far-reaching and detailed technical investigation ever carried out on an aircraft, the Comet reappeared in redesigned and strengthened form in 1958. Results of the searching tests and stringent investigation of earlier versions were freely made available to manufacturers all over the world. These findings influenced design details on many modern jets.

Below:
Boeing Stratocruisers were used on the New York service from 1949.

The first two Comet 4s were handed over to BOAC on 30 September 1958 after an intensive period of preparation. Four days later a Comet left London and another left New York, simultaneously inaugurating the world's first transatlantic pure-jet commercial service. Schedule for the westbound flight was 10¼hr, almost halving the earlier piston-engined Stratocruiser times.

Above:
The Canadair C-54GM Argonaut was Rolls-Royce Merlin engined Dougla DC-4, first introduced in August 1949.

Below:
Unfortunately the Comet 1's triumphant introduction in May 1952 was short-lived.
British Airways Collection (courtesy the RAF Museum)

The pattern of BOAC services was augmented in 1960 when the South American route, closed since 1954, was reopened on 25 January with Comets. Argonauts, which had given excellent service during their long life, were retired on 8 April. In nearly 11 years they had flown approximately 107 million miles and carried 870,000 passengers. Government approval had been given to BOAC in October 1956 to buy 15 Boeing 707s. On 27 May 1960 a London-New York service was opened with these new, large, high-speed aircraft — the first of the long-range, high-capacity jet generation. They steadily took over on the North Atlantic until on 16 October the Comet 4 fleet was retired from this route.

Looking to the future, BOAC signed a

contract in January 1958 for 35 Standard VC10 airliners with an option on a further 20. In June 1960 an additional order for 10 Super VC10s was signed.

In 1960, for the first time in six years, BOAC was able to face its task with confidence. It had the right aircraft, the long, essential experience and had staked out its future. Traffic prospects — especially cargo — were good. But in the world of commerce nothing is simple. BOAC had calculated its required capacity on a rate of traffic growth based on past statistics and estimation of future demands. In 1961 it stood ready to meet this need.

But quite suddenly, and for no obvious reason, revenue traffic fell off. The upward slope of the graph flattened out and every major airline company found itself with too little traffic to fill its extra capacity. BOAC, still in its final stages of recovery from the Comet disasters, had 33% more space in 1961 than in the year before. But its increase of revenue traffic was 9%, producing only 5½% more revenue. In the face of what amounted to a recession in airline business the book value of older aircraft in the fleet, Comets, Britannias and DC-7s fell faster

Below:
Douglas DC-7Cs were introduced as a stop-gap in 1957, pending the delivery of the delayed Britannia fleet.
British Airways Collection (courtesy the RAF Museum)

than allowed for by the Corporation. Accordingly their values had to be written off by £33 million in one year. This, together with operating losses, brought BOAC's accumulated deficit to £64 million at the end of the 1961/62 financial year.

BOAC's policy of technical help and financial support to overseas associated companies in the Middle East and Far East, African and the West Atlantic, in which BOAC's investments in 1963 totalled £2million, had not been without its disappointments. In the 1961/62 year these investments cost BOAC a highest ever £3.4 million in losses made by these associated companies; and in the next fiscal year £840,000. But the help given enabled local air services to be maintained in the developing countries where they might otherwise have failed.

In the succeeding financial year — 1962/63 — BOAC's results were a little better. After interest had been paid on all capital there was a loss of £12.9 million compared with £14.4 million in the year before. It was the second year of traffic stalemate. Receipts were slightly lower than the previous year but total expenditure was cut and losses by associated companies reduced. The accumulated deficit reached a total of £77 million. But, in spite of short-term financial difficulties, the operational future was not forgotten. During 1962, following arrangements between Britain and France to build a supersonic airliner — the Concorde —

BOAC agreed to purchase a number of these transports if they met a specified pattern of performance.

Towards the end of the 1950s, cargo, which had been following a steady if unspectacular growth pattern, began suddenly to leap ahead. Long term selling pressures by all airlines were partly responsible together with increasing awareness in industry of the advantages of air freighting. By mid-1960 BOAC's cargo traffic had settled down to a hitherto unprecedented rate of increase. It averaged 27% a year over four years and showed little signs of slackening after this.

On the North Atlantic, demand for cargo space was particularly heavy. Two DC-7F cargo aircraft, converted from BOAC DC-7C passenger aircraft, first put into service on this route on 3 December 1960 were followed in October 1963 by a Canadair CL44 swing-tail cargo freighter under lease. Much of the cargo traffic continued to be carried in the holds of passenger aircraft but two large-capacity Boeing 707-336C freighters were ordered for North Atlantic traffic. In 1963/64 freight accounted for 9.5% of the total BOAC revenue.

An event of some significance occurred in June 1962 when BOAC and the Cunard Steam-Ship Co became associated. By agreement a new company, BOAC-Cunard Ltd became responsible for a large proportion of British ar services across the Atlantic. Its combined abilities were concentrated into serving the US eastern seaboard and mid-west, Bermuda, the Bahamas, the Caribbean together with the extension of those services to parts of northern and western South America. Initial capital of the new company was £30 million of which BOAC contributed 70% and Cunard 30%. The aim was to offer the best-known British transport systems in a combined attack on the American travel and commercial markets.

During 1963 there were all-round improvements in traffic revenue, load factors and financial results. They resulted in a significant and encouraging 1963/64 annual report. It showed that for the first time revenue had exceeded £100 million in a year, increasing by 12.3% over the previous year. At the same time, expenditure had been cut by 3.5%. The operating profit reached a record high level of £8.7 million, leaving, for the first time for seven years, a surplus after paying interest on all capital employed. But clearly there had been disquiet in the mind of the Minister of Aviation over the past performance of BOAC. During 1962 he had appointed Mr John Corbett to conduct a confidential examination of BOAC's accounts and financial prospects. The result of this enquiry was presented to the Minister but not revealed publicly in detail. But a White Paper, 'The Financial Problems of the British Overseas Airways Corporation', that drew on the Corbett report, was published in November 1963. Its general tone was critical of some parts of the BOAC organisation and a number of its past decisions.

A summary of events leading up to the unprofitable years in the early 1960s was later clearly detailed in a report of the Select Committee on Nationalised Industries published in June 1964. It revealed for the first time some of the pressures to which BOAC had been subjected. But the Minister of Aviation had in mind some form of reorganisation for BOAC and as a result both the chairman, Sir Matthew Slattery and the managing director, Sir Basil Smallpiece, resigned in 1963. The minister appointed Sir Giles Guthrie chairman and he took up that position on 1 January 1964. Acting also as chief executive, he at once got down to a critical examination of the airline and began preparing a plan that would help to establish profitable operations in the future. The board of BOAC was reorganised and a clear directive given by the minister on the future responsibilities of the airline.

Sir Giles's plan was unfolded in stages through the year. The first part was a study of the current and future prospects of the routes that BOAC flew. From this part of the plan emerged the decision to terminate the unprofitable service to Washington and the loss-making route down the east coast of South America. The second stage of the plan covered the

Left:
The medium range Britannia 102 was used for African services from late 1955.

Below:
The stretched Britannia 312 started trans-Atlantic services in December 1957.

Bottom:
Comet 4s had replaced the Britannias in less than a year on the New York service.

aircraft fleet required to operate the route network. It became apparent that the six-year old study on which was based the order for the VC10 fleet was now unrealistic. After negotiations, the British Government allowed BOAC to modify its order for 12 standard and 30 Super versions of the VC10 but limited the change to 12 standard and 17 Super with 10 remaining 'in suspense' and the remaining three going to the RAF. BOAC had wanted, after its study, to be relieved of the necessity for accepting any of the 30 Super VC10s.

On 1 April 1965 Sir Giles was able to announce a profit of £7 million after deducting tax, interest on capital and other charges. However interest payments on capital had grown to such a size that they prevented BOAC from building up much-needed reserves. Under the Air Corporations Act 1966 a total of £130 million capital was written off. New capital liabilities amounting to £66 million were created. Of this total, £35 million was called 'exchequer dividend capital' on which BOAC was to pay dividends when results enabled it to do so.

On 1 April 1967 BOAC became the first airline to operate two distinct round-the-world routes, when it opened a South Pacific route between Australia and Britain. The route linked Sydney to San Francisco via Fiji and Honolulu. In the same year work was begun on BOAC's new £5 million cargo terminal at Heathrow, which was officially opened in May 1970 by HRH The Duke of Edinburgh.

In May 1969 a new Polar route to Japan was opened. Boeing 707-336C airliners flew from London non-stop to Anchorage and then on to Tokyo and Osaka. The route to Japan was shortened even further when on 2 June 1970 a London-Moscow-Tokyo service was inaugurated, also with 336Cs. Both these services provided new round-the-world routeings.

By 31 March 1970 BOAC had completed six years of record profit making and was able to announce that it no longer owed the Government a penny. By this time delivery of the first of the 'wide-bodied' generation of aircraft was beginning and BOAC received the first of the 12 Boeing 747 'Jumbo Jets' ordered in 1966.

It was becoming clear that the longer term future of the airline would lie in consolidation of the fleet into one or two wide-bodied aircraft types, with the addition of a supersonic long range aircraft with considerably fewer seats and interest was being taken in the development of the Anglo-French Concorde, then undergoing trials. At the same time the Committee of Inquiry into Civil Air Transport in Britain,

Above left:
A large fleet of VC10s was ordered in 1958, but only 12 of this 'standard' version were delivered.

Left:
Boeing 707s, ordered in 1956, took over the trans-Atlantic services in October 1960.

Below:
This Super VC10 carries the titles BOAC-Cunard, the joint company set up in June 1962.

under the chairmanship of Professor Sir Ronald Edwards, was reporting its recommendations to the Government for changes to currrent civil aviation policy.

The Report of the Committee of Inquiry was published in May 1969. The General Conclusion of the Report (Cmd 4018 HMSO) recommended *inter alia* formation of a National Air Holdings Board, under which BOAC and BEA would each retain their separate identities but be subject to financial control in the widest interests; formation of a 'second force' airline, broadly to cover operations then catered for by a miscellany of private companies; a consortium of regional airlines within British Air Services on a mixed ownership basis and formation of a

Civil Aviation Authority which would be a semi-autonomous authority devoted to holding and strengthening Britain's place in world aviation.

Following debate and discussion on the Report, the British Airways Board was set up by the Civil Aviation Act 1971. Under this act the board assumed ownership and control of BEA and BOAC. One of the first duties of the board was to review all the activities grouped under its control with the object of determining whether these were organised in the most efficient way. By July 1972 the board had decided upon an initial structure designed to provide unified direction and control of all units within British Airways.

Studies by the board resulted in three main Reports to Parliament concerning the future organisation. Broadly, the first report proposed that there should be seven operating divisions. The second report recommended adoption of a single brand name 'British Airways' for all trading and operational purposes. The third report recommended dissolution of BEA and BOAC. All the reports were accepted and approved by the Government and British Airways, as a single entity, came into being on 1 April 1974. After nearly 35 years British Overseas Airways Corporation disappeared from public view, swallowed up by the re-emergence of British Airways. Although BOAC vanished its memory and the Speedbird insignia has lingered on as a fitting tribute to those pioneering years.

Reproduced from **Highways in the air**, *courtesy British Airways PLC.*

Above left:
Boeing 707s were used for the expanding cargo business in the 1960s.

Below:
BOAC's last aircraft to enter service was the Boeing 747, of which 12 had been ordered in 1966.

Belgium's Brilliant Biplane

Edwin A. Shackleton

The Stampe SV4 owes its origins to a Belgian, Jeam Stampe, who was born in 1889. Whilst serving in the Belgian Army in World War 1, he volunteered for flying duties and was sent, at the age of 27, to Hendon for flying training. After the hostilities he was personal pilot to King Albert 1 but resigned in 1922 to form his own flying school in association with Maurice Vertongen, ex-wartime pilot and financier. Due to the lack of suitable aircraft, they employed Alfred Renard to design their trainers which materialised into the Renard Stampe and Vertongen RSV32, RSV26, RSV18 and RSV22. The numbers referred to the wing area in square metres. Some 93 machines of these types were built before Renard left to form his own company. He was replaced by Georges Ivanow

and in the same year, Stampe et Vertongen became agents for de Havilland and they purchased 11 Moths and a Puss Moth.

The most significant design of the company appeared in 1933. Originally known as the S1V but soon as the SV4 it was obviously influenced by the Moth design but bore its own proud lines. The Gypsy-powered prototype of all-wood construction registered OO-ANI, with straight lower wing and swept upper wing, made its maiden flight on 17 May 1933 in the hands of Jean Stampe. The second flight, two days later, was carried out by his 24-year old son, who was to perish a year later with Georges Ivanow in the only SV10 twin-engined bomber. A further five SV4s were built for service with the Stampe et Vertongen flying school.

Further development took place under engineer Demidoff, utilising the Gypsy Major, installing ailerons on the upper wing, modifying the empennage and eventually sweeping the lower wing.

After a competition in July 1939, Jean Stampe gained an order for 30 aircraft, designated SV4B, for the Belgian Flying Corps. The first machine was completed at Antwerp in December 1939 while the last of the total batch of 30 was delivered on 13 May 1940, just three days after the German invasion of Belgium. Fortunately, 24 Stampes were loaded on to a cargo ship destined for Oran in North Africa, and saw useful service. One of the earlier civil aircraft, OO-ATD, was stored in a shed at the

Left:
Jean Stampe in full flying gear, posing alongside a DH Moth from his flying school.
Photo via Maj Roger Hanington

Above right:
The prototype all-wood construction SV4 00-ANI flown by Jean Stampe in 1933.
Photo via Maj Roger Hanington

Right:
A line-up of 11 SV4Bs for the Belgian Flying Corps in 1940. The under-wing hoops were a feature of this initial batch. *Photo via Maj Roger Hanington*

Chateau Ter-Block. It became the centre of attention for two Belgian Air Force NCOs Michel Donnet and Leon Divoy. For three months they worked in great secrecy until it was deemed airworthy. Their first engine run on the night of 4 July 1941 led them straight into an escape flight through anti-aircraft fire, to cross the English Channel and a safe landing at Thorpe-le-Soken, Essex.

This Stampe served in a communications role during World War 2 and has now found a final and worthy resting place in the Belgian Military Museum in Brussels.

Meanwhile the French government had placed an order for 300 SV4s, six days after the start of World War 2. It was quite obvious that this order could not be fulfilled by Stampe et Vertongen at their small factory and so the French nationalised Farman company was licensed to produce most of the batch. This order was raised to 600 aircraft of which 50 were to be produced in Belgium. The Belgian-built aircraft were to be powered by the 132hp Gypsy Major 2 and the Farman-built machines would be fitted with the 140hp Renault 4Pei. Only 10

of these were actually completed due to the German advance. No machines appear to have been built in France before WW2.

In 1944, the French Ministry of Defence ordered 1,400 SV4 trainers. Farman had not resumed aircraft production and manufacture was placed with Societe Nationale Aeronautique du Nord (SNCAN). The order was revised to 700 when RAF surplus Tiger Moths were acquired to meet Armée de l'Air requirements. The production rate was so rapid that the first aircraft flew on 4 June 1945 and just over 400 were constructed in 1946. The total order of 700 was completed in 1949. Jean Stampe, who had spent the war period in Paris, flew the first postwar Stampe on its second flight.

He returned to his home country where the factory at Antwerp had been destroyed and met Alfred Renard who had designed the early RSV trainers. They formed a joint company, Stampe et Renard on 13 February 1947, to resume production of the SV4. The prewar SV4B was improved by the installation of a 145hp DH Gypsy Major 10 engine, and also an enclosed

Above:
Stampe SV4As were flown by the *Patrouille d'Etampes* from 1947 to 1953. This example was photographed at White Waltham in 1950.
Edwin Shackleton

Below:
The Belgian Air Force team *Les Manchots* (the Penguins) flew Stampes modified with an enclosed rear cockpit, like these examples flying a mirror formation.

perspex canopy. The Belgian Air Force ordered a batch of 65 trainers, the first of which was flown by Jean Stampe on 22 June 1948, the last one flying seven years later. A final, 66th Stampe was built for company use. The Air Force aircraft were maintained by Stampe et Renard. Jean Stampe flew the last aeroplane to complete a major servicing at his company in 1968 when he reached the grand age of 79. He remained active until 1971, then aged 82, when the Stampe et Renard Company closed down.

The production batch of 700 Stampes proved insufficient for French military requirements and as SNCA du Nord was committed on other programmes, an order for 150 Stampe SV4Cs was placed with the Algerian company, l'Atelier Industriel de l'Air d'Alger in 1947. This batch benefited from the use of the local Algerian ash which was of superior quality. The last Stampe from the Algerian line flew in 1950. The French Naval Air Service (Aeronavale) and Army Aviation (ALAT) operated the Stampe SV4, the majority being received from the Air Force as their requirements diminished. The French Air Force aerobatic team, the *Patrouille d'Etampes* was reformed in June 1947 with six Stampe SV4A biplanes powered by Renault 4P05 engines with inverted oil and fuel systems. It was hoped to equip these Stampes with 175hp Mathis, seven-cylinder radial engines, but the sole conversion, the SV4D, proved unreliable. The *Patrouille* continued with its SV4As until September 1953.

Eleven years later, the Belgian Air Force formed its own aerobatic team called *Les Manchots* (the Penguins) with three SV4Bs which were specially modified with a small canopy over the rear cockpit. They remained in service until 1968 when the Stampes were replaced in the training role by the SIAI Marchetti SF260.

Above:
The first Stampe to be operated in the UK was SV4B F-BDGQ which became G-AROZ with the Tiger Club in 1962.

Below:
These Stampes equipped the original Rothmans Aerobatic Team between 1970 and 1972.
Photo via Rothmans of Pall Mall

The postwar French governments were keen to promote civil aviation and one of their actions was to promote national flying centres and aerobatic training where the Stampe found a particular niche. These biplanes were also used for parachuting and glider towing although the latter role highlighted some limitations.

The Stampe SV4 had established itself as a responsive aerobatic machine with good handling characteristics. It achieved honour at the International Aerobatic Contest at Coventry in August 1955 when Frenchman Leon Biancotto took first place, winning the Lockheed Trophy and £500 prize money in his Stampe SV4C, F-BCFA and his fellow countryman Francois d'Huc-Dressler came third in the same machine.

It was not until 1962, that the first Stampe was imported into the UK. It had become obvious that the Tiger Moth was not comparable to its French rival despite modifications carried out by Rollasons of Croydon for the Tiger Club. As a result the Stampe SV4B, F-BDGQ was bought by Norman Jones for the Tiger Club becoming G-AROZ and appropriately named *Leon Biancotto*. The Stampe has since remained a significant part of the British aerobatic scene although gradually being pushed into the background by the more agile Pitts Specials and the sophisticated specially designed monoplanes such as the Stephens Akro.

The Rothmans Aerobatic Team brought the Stampe to the notice of the British public. Manx Kelly had retired from 19 years serivce in the Royal Air Force with the dream of forming his own aerobatic team. Fortunately, this coincided with Rothmans of Pall Mall seeking something totally new to revitilise their sponsorship programme. The result was a search for four suitable aircraft and the formation of a team. In just three months from initial negotiations, the first public appearance took place in May 1970 at Blackbushe, followed by another 40 shows that year. In 1971, they carried out 70 displays and Manx Kelly also became the British Aerobatic Champion. The Stampes served for another year but were then replaced by the Pitts

Below:
Although registered as G-BHFG this SNCAN SV4C is painted in the markings it carried with the French Navy.

Right:
SV4A G-OODE was owned by a French aerobatic champion before coming to this country for display work with Richard Goode. It is now flown by Vic Norman from Kemble.

S-2A. Manx Kelly's team in 1970 was Iain Weston, Neil Williams and Roy Hogarth, later pilots being Barry Tempest, Mike Thompson, Rod Freeman and Mike Findlay.

The Stampe was also used for solo aerobatic displays over the years. Perhaps the leading exponent today is Brian Lecomber who also flies his Pitts Special but finds pleasure in the more sedate artistry of the older Stampe. His aircraft is an Algerian-built SV4C with a Renault engine but it has since been modified to be powered by a 150hp Gypsy Major 10.

The Stampe has been used many times in film roles, sometimes camouflaged to represent the fighters of past years, rather inadequately. However, major conversions of a few Stampes were carried out by Personal Plane Services to 'mimic' Royal Aircraft Factory SE5As for the film *Blue Max*. This was achieved by completely new cowlings, cockpit surround and fin/rudder shapes, which resulted in very convincing side elevations.

The Tiger Club, who imported the first Stampe, still continue to operate two Stampe SV4Bs either for the use of their members or for public display, perhaps in formation with Tiger Moths (to confuse the uninitiated), Turbulents or in their impeccable mirror formation.

Many private individuals operate their own Stampes as sporting aircraft where they enjoy open cockpit flying and are able to perform their own aerobatic routine. Some 70 Stampes have been imported into Britain in the last 22 years

and 46 are currently registered. About 25 are now airworthy but this number is constantly changing as restoration or rebuilding activities proceed.

A recent innovation was the formation of the UK Stampe Club whose aim is to act as the focus for the interest of owners, pilots and enthusiasts, to encourage interest and to spread knowledge of the aeroplane. It has already arranged flying and social meetings, bringing together those with common aims.

Total production of the Stampe SV4 · in Belgium, France and Algeria was 977 from 1933 until 1955 and it is believed that about 200 are still active. It was, undoubtedly, the most successful aircraft either designed or built in Belgium and was also one of the classic biplane trainers of the World, sharing honours with the Tiger Moth and Stearman, Avro 504 and Curtiss Jenny . . . and it looks set to grace our skies for many years to come.

Above:
Built in Belgium postwar, SV4B G-DANN features an enclosed cockpit canopy.

Right:
Mirror formation by two Tiger Club Stampes. The inverted aircraft is Algerian built and imported in 1965 while its French built 'reflection' was brought in three years later.

Tante Ju

Roger Wright

The aviation enthusiast has witnessed a rebirth of aircraft in the air display sector of aviation over the past five years for, during that period, the number and variety of aeroplanes from the WW2 era has trebled. Today the re-emergence of obsolete machines, believed long gone, is a regular occurrence which is now being taken for granted.

Aircraft participation at many of the summer's air shows often manages to include a fair selection of Warbirds' representatives of the Allied Forces in WW2, often including at least one example of the legendary Douglas DC-3 Dakota. It was exciting therefore to witness the emergence of the Dak's contemporary — the Junkers Ju52/3M — on to the UK show circuit two years ago, to represent the Luftwaffe in the battle scenes. This large, lumbering, three-engined transport aircraft, which represents the backbone of Hitler's mighty aerial war machine is in fact a Spanish-built CASA 352, a license-built derivative of the German-designed Junkers Ju52 which, like the DC-3, was initially designed as a medium/long range passenger airliner, in the early 1930s.

The Ju52 in fact began life as a single-engined aircraft, the prototype of which made its maiden flight on 13 October 1930. An extensive series of flight tests were carried out, combined with the installation of six alternative types of engine. But conclusive results proved the design to be underpowered, necessitating the adaption and evaluation of the 7th air frame to a three-engined configuration. The beginning of 1931 saw the mating of three Pratt & Whitney 550hp Hornet radial engines and, on 14 April 1931, the trimotor version designated Ju52/3mce-made its maiden flight.

Orders for the aircraft were quickly received from operators in Belgium, Finland and Sweden in addition to the German national airline Lufthansa. In May 1932, some 13 months after the maiden flight, Lufthansa commenced commercial operations with the 15-17 seat aircraft, the vanguard of over 240 Ju52s delivered to the airline, representing 80% of the prewar fleet.

Two of Professor Hugo Junkers main design features were incorporated into the aircraft's design, namely an all-metal corrugated skin, first employed some 17 years previously on the world's first all-metal aeroplane — the Junkers J1. The second feature was the now famous Junkers 'double wing' that comprised full span flaps with ailerons hinged below the trailing edge of the main wing. These innovations gave the aircraft a short-field take-off/landing capability and combined with the high lift wing that spanned 96ft, it gave an approach speed of only 60mph fully loaded. Severe icing problems were commonplace, however, on the flap/aileron sections and without doubt this contributed greatly to the high rate of attrition on the Russian Front.

The short-field capability of the Ju52 was also assisted by the powerplants, the aircraft being adequately powered; virtually 95% of the 4,845 aircraft built were fitted with the 725hp 132A or larger 830hp 132T BMW nine-cylinder radial engine. One engine was situated in the nose on the centreline and one on each wing, installed at right-angles to the leading edge of the tapered wing, giving a splayed out appearance in relation to the line of the fuselage.

Rebirth of the Luftwaffe under Herman Goring in 1935 brought about the construction of Ju52s in substantial numbers, initially as 'bombers', that were used with some effect in the Spanish Civil War, and subsequently as the mainstay of the tactical transport force carrying parachutists and their equipment. The aeroplane was constructed in 14 different versions and, due to its robustness and adaptability, participated with significance on every front on which the Nazi forces fought including the Low Countries, Norway, Russia and Eastern Europe, North Africa. For example, during Operation 'Mercury' almost 500 Ju52s took part in both para-dropping, supply flying and as glider tugs in the Balkans and Crete.

The end of hostilities in Europe also brought about the virtual demise of the German-built trimotor transporter with the exception of those

Tante Ju en route to a display in mid-1984

Left:
This angle shows the splayed out line of the port and starboard radial engines. *Roger Wright*

This page:
The unusual rugged lines of the Ju52 trimotor are revealed in these air to air shots. *Roger Wright*

that formed the heavy transport component of the Swiss Air Force. Production numbers totalling 4,845 at the end of WW2 including aircraft assembled in France and Hungary during 1942-44. Postwar construction of the design under license was continued in Europe. In France Amiot built 400 for Air France and

the French Air Force (designated AAC-1s), and 170 were constructed by Construcciones Aeronauticas, Spain as CASA 352Ls for the Spanish Air Force in whose hands they were designated T-2Bs, for use as multi-role transports. The remnants of this fleet remained operational until the mid-1970s.

Following withdrawal from service most of the CASA 352s were reduced to scrap. A small number however were retained in airworthy condition and placed in reserve in March 1976 for a three year period until final disposal, mostly to private collections. *Tante Ju*, the subject of this article, was one of this batch and, following acquisition, spent the next seven years stored at Malaga Airport in Spain.

Occasional trips were made from the UK during this time to maintain the aircraft in a

On display at North Weald

Below:
The gunner has a draughty job during the display.
Andrew March

general state of serviceability, but lack of finance excluded any form of serious maintenance. In February 1983, however, a consortium was formed entitled the 'Junkers Ju52/3M Flight' with the intention of restoring the aircraft to flying condition. Finance for the project was forthcoming and in June 1983 a maintenance team went to Spain to prepare the aircraft for a ferry flight to Britain.

A combination of high temperatures and low humidity in Spain proved sympathetic to the 36-year old aircraft, that had flown a total of 4,300hr since entering service with the Spanish Air Force in March 1947. Inspections of the airframe and flying controls provided no evidence of corrosion and, with the exception of normal maintenance problems due largely to the lack of lubrication, the team were totally satisfied with the overall condition of the T-2B

Tante Ju retained her original Emna Beta nine-cylinder air-cooled radial engines, each requiring large amounts of time and money to bring them to a fit standard for the ferry flight. However, following six exhaustive weeks of

hard work, and following FAA certification, the CASA 352 now registered N9012P, made the lengthy flight to the UK. Flown by John 'Jeff' Hawke it arrived in time to make its show debut at West Malling at the end of September 1983.

The following winter encompassed a long and detailed programme of maintenance work on the Ju52 at the Flight's home base at Rochester Airport, Kent. Simplicity of the aircraft's electrical systems and its flying controls that operate by means of a push-rod system that eliminates hydraulics, permitted time and money for necessary engine repairs and works. The ageing engines were removed and a complete overhaul carried out. This required the replacement of ignition systems, magnetos, generators and starter units. Fortunately the group had secured a large selection of spares during the period in Spain, together with one complete overhauled engine, which ensured the aircraft's serviceability for the 1984 season.

Refurbishment of the aircraft involved stripping it back to bare metal prior to a complete respray both inside and outside. The Aerospace Museum, Cosford came to the Flight's rescue exchanging two virtually new main wheel tyres for the original ones which had been in very bad condition. It was during this period of refurbishment that the internal section of the

rear upper turret was discovered intact, with the fuselage top merely plated over. A gun mounting of similar design to the original was fitted and a machine gun modified to operate on oxygen and Calor gas was installed to give a touch of authenticity.

May 1984 saw the aircraft's emergence on to the air display circuit commencing at Biggin Hill Air Fair. It was now authentically painted in the two-tone green splinter camouflage represensentative of a Ju52 serving with 2nd Staffel, KGxb VI (Battle Wing for Special Duties) based in the Balkans during 1941.

The Ju52/3M appeared at 26 displays during its first season and continued last year during the 50th anniversary year of her contemporary, the Douglas DC-3 Dakota. One wonders how many people actually realise that *Tante Ju* celebrated her 50th birthday four years previously and, but for the War, the type might have matched the production totals of the Dak. The only reason precluding her from matching the Dakota was that *Tante Ju* simply 'finished her War on the wrong side'.

Below:
He might end up on the receiving end in a 'warbird scene', as this Spitfire runs in to attack the 'Luftwaffe' aircraft.

Right:
The spartan interior of the CASA 352L with its folding para seats. *Roger Wright*

Bournemouth-Hurn Airport

Peter R. March

Covering almost 1,000 acres the airfield at Hurn was constructed as a military airfield during the early years of WW2, although the site had earlier been identified by Sir Alan Cobham as suitable for an airport. He had been commissioned in the 1930s by Bournemouth Corporation to recommend the best location for their proposed Municipal Airport and subsequently used it for his well known Air Circus and other flying activities.

Construction of the airfield started in 1940 and by the following March it was well advanced with runways and some of the dispersal pens complete. Squadron offices, a watch office and armoury were under construction, and the four domestic sites around Hurn village already had accommodation for about 600 men. Hurn opened as a satellite to Ibsley in July 1941, but was only used occasionally by that station's aircraft prior to the arrival of the Special Duty

Right:
Sir Alan Cobham who first identified the site at Hurn for an airfield. *Aerofilms*

Below:
The airfield saw many military aircraft pressed into service for civil operations like this Whitley V.
British Airways Collection

Flight from Christchurch in November 1941. Its miscellaneous collection was used for radar trials by the Telecommunications Research Establishment at Swanage.

A detachment of Liberators from 1425 Flight, Honeybourne, arrived at the end of the year, but both it and the Telecommunications Flying Unit (SDF renamed) had gone by the end of May 1942 in readiness for Hurn's first major job — as a 38 Wing, AAC base. No 297 Squadron brought its Whitleys during June and continued paratroop exercises, two months later being joined by the similarly equipped No 296 Squadron. Both units commenced 'nickelling' over France before leaving at short notice on 25 October 1942. This was for the build-up in North Africa after Operation 'Torch' when Hurn, with other airfields in the south, was used as a departure point for units flying out en masse.

No 296 Squadron returned from Andover on 19 December to join 1458 (TT) Flight which had formed at Hurn earlier in the month with Lysanders. Night towing of Horsas commenced in January 1943 and the following month the first Albemarles arrived, the squadron being completely re-equipped by the end of May. The Albemarle, an aircraft rejected for the bomber

Above:
BOAC moved in with its Dakotas like G-AGHE from Whitchurch in November 1944.
British Airways Collection

Below:
Until the 1960s BOAC continued to use Hurn for crew training.

Top:
The first aircraft to be built at Hurn was the Vickers Varsity in 1952-53.

Above:
Two-thirds of the 444 Viscounts were built by Vickers at Hurn, including this example operated by the Omani Air Force.

role, found its niche as a glider tug, proving well able to cope with a loaded Horsa or Hadrian. The first operational flight was on 9 February when an Albemarle dropped leaflets on Lisieux, Normandy, and this was followed strangely in view of its earlier rejection, by bombing attacks.

In June 1943 the squadron left for Froka, Algeria, in preparation for Operation 'Beggar', the invasion of Sicily. For the same operation No 295 Squadron used Halifaxes which had been modified at Hurn for glider towing by a working party from 13 MU, while the Heavy Glider Maintenance Unit prepared the Horsas. No 295 Squadron collected the combinations from Hurn at the beginning of June and flew them to Portreath, ready for the long flight to North Africa.

No 296 Squadron returned from the Middle East in October, to be joined by part of No 295. The latter converted to Albemarles and built up to squadron strength, while in November No 570 Squadron was formed with the same aircraft. All three squadrons then undertook a heavy training programme, and also did supply drops over France, despatching arms and equipment to the Maquis.

For 'Overlord' the 38 Group units moved further inland, giving up Hurn to 11 Group on 15 March 1944. No 125 Squadron moved its Mosquito NF XVIIs down from Valley and immediately found itself involved on Operation 'Eric', supporting decoy bombing raids drop-

Top:
An early production BAC 1-11 for British United Airways after a test flight at Hurn.

Above:
The last BAC1-11, G-BLHD, was delivered just before the British Aerospace factory closed down in June 1984.

ping 'window'. On 18 March 143 Wing, consisting of Nos 438, 439 and 440 (RCAF) Squadrons, arrived fresh from fighter training at Ayr. All three squadrons had flown their first sweeps by the end of the month and their Typhoons were soon a regular sight over the Cherbourg peninsula. They went to Funtington for dive bombing training, exchanging places with 124 Wing whose squadrons, Nos 181, 182 and 247, concentrated on rocket firing.

No 143 Wing returned to Hurn later in April, and the six squadrons started full scale operations over France, attacking 'Noball' sites and bridges. No 438 Squadron became the first Typhoon unit to drop 1,000lb bombs operationally, and from 10 May an all-out offensive was begun on radar stations along the French coast. Meanwhile No 604 Squadron had joined the Hurn-based units on 3 May to strengthen the 85 Group Mosquito night fighter force in

readiness for D-Day. During the last major night raid on Britain, on 15/16 May 1944, No 125 Squadron shot down a Ju88 near Cherbourg and 604 got a Ju188. A week later, despite only spasmodic activity by the Luftwaffe, 125 was able to claim another Ju88 and a '188 in the Southampton area.

All squadrons were on alert for operations on D-Day, the night fighters having started covering Allied forces during the previous night. During 6/7 June No 604 Squadron shot down five enemy aircraft, and another five on

the 8th. This extraordinary success included two He177s, but it obviously could not be sustained and indeed night activity dropped off considerably as the month progressed. However, standing patrols over the beachhead at the end of June netted No 125 Squadron four destroyed and one damaged in three nights, the unit then transferring to 'Anti-Diver' patrols and leaving Hurn.

The six weeks prior to D-Day had resulted in heavy losses for the Typhoon squadrons, and

Above:
Sea Fury FB11 WG536 of the Fleet Requirements Unit landing at Hurn in September 1960.

Below:
These distinctive black-painted Sea Hawks were operated by the FRU in the 60s.

the all-out attacks on German armour which followed did not provide any respite. On 20 June 124 Wing moved to the continent and was replaced at Hurn by Nos 164, 198 and 609 Squadrons (136 Wing). 143 Wing also moved to France to keep the cab rank going and by the end of the month all 83 Group Typhoons were on the Continent.

All three 84 Group Typhoon Wings, 123, 136 and 146, now consolidated at Hurn, the squadrons flying daily to landing strips in France to carry out sweeps, attacking railway communications in the German rear areas. During July they gradually moved to France, leaving No 183 Squadron to attack the remaining German coastal radar sites.

After a short visit by 418 (RCAF) Squadron with its intruder Mosquito VIs, Hurn was suddenly empty. But not for long, for on

5 August the B-26 Marauders of the 397th Bomb Group arrived from Rivenhall for operations over France. An attack on the rail marshalling yards at Corbiel provided them with their most impressive results when their first bombs hit trucks loaded with explosives, and sympathetic detonations destroyed the whole complex. The units moved to France as soon as an airfield became available, but the USAAF retained Hurn for another month.

Handed back in October, the airfield was taken over by BOAC, who transferred their main landplane base from Whitchurch on 1 November 1944. The airfield has already been used for some BOAC flights but these now increased markedly as routes across France became available. The airfield was transferred to the Ministry of Civil Aviation and BOAC was joined by KLM and Sabena, and before long by Pan American and American Overseas Airways who started the first regular landplane services from the United States. The airport was very busy during the immediate postwar era but on 1 January 1946 London Airport opened and the services were gradually transferred. The BOAC Development Flight and some maintenance work continued at Hurn which was also used for crew training, but by the mid-1950s it was very run-down.

During 1951 Vickers-Armstrong Ltd took over one of the old BOAC hangars on the north side and used the airfield for flight testing the prototype Valiants while a runway was laid at Wisley. Production of the Varsity was then

Below:
The last of the Navy's Scimitars also served with the FRU at Hurn.

Bottom:
One of the most familiar airliners to operate from Hurn over the years has been the Herald. This example is in the colours of Jersey Airlines.

transferred from Weybridge and, with more factory buildings completed, a Viscount line was established.

The first Hurn-built Viscount flew in December 1953 and production rapidly rose to six aircraft a month with sales all over the world. The British Aircraft Corporation at Hurn built more short haul turbine powered aircraft than any other factory in the western world and of the 444 Viscounts built, many of which are still in service, nearly two-thirds came from Hurn.

As Viscount production declined Hurn produced parts for the Vanguard and the VC10 and Super VC10 intercontinental jets. At the end of 1961 Hurn prepared for the production of the BAC 1-11 and by October 1962, the first fuselage was complete, the first maiden flight taking place on 20 August 1963 at a time when the second and third 1-11s were already in final assembly and the twelth fuselage was being built. Production of the 1-11, through the advanced 500 and 475 series, continued at the airport, latterly in connection with the very valuable contract with Rumania. In addition to the construction of complete aircraft, the Hurn factory also produced parts for the Concorde, including wiring looms, thermal and sound insulation, and complete nose sections together with other civil and military aircraft work. Sadly the recession of the late 1970s and early 1980s

Right:
Silver City's car ferry to Cherbourg used this Freighter 32 G-ANWL for several years.

Below:
Services to the Channel Islands have been operated by a number of companies including Metropolitan using this Hurn-based Islander G-BCEN.

and the privatisation and rationalisation of British Aerospace plc resulted in a decision to close the Hurn factory by mid-1984. The last BAC1-11 was delivered in May and the doors finally shut on the factory in June that year.

In 1952 Airwork Services Ltd formed a Fleet Requirements Unit for the Admiralty, unique in having civilian aircrews flying Service aircraft. The unit worked its way through most postwar naval types, starting with the Mosquito and Sea Hornet, and ending with the Hunter and Canberra. On 1 December 1972 the Airwork FRU was amalgamated with the Air Direction Training Unit at Yeovilton and consolidated at HMS *Heron* as the Fleet Requirements and Air Direction Unit.

During the 1960s Hurn's traffic reached nearly 15,000 air transport movements (ie passenger and/or cargo flights), 250,000 passengers and 20,000,000kg freight per annum. The Ministry of Aviation which then owned both Southampton and Hurn Airports designated the latter as the airport to be developed to serve the South of England and planned improvements included a new terminal building to be built in the north-east corner of the airfield at a cost of over £250,000. During this period destinations

served included Cherbourg, Paris, Belgium, Holland and Switzerland, and Glasgow and Edinburgh were included in the domestic network; Hurn was one of the busiest airports in the country.

The late 1960s, the last years of Government ownership of the airport, saw a considerable decline in passenger and freight, with airport hours reduced to 09.00-17.00 Monday to Friday and this was the situation obtaining when the Bournemouth and Dorset Councils took over ownership of the airport on 1 April 1969.

During the 1970s the airport made a slow, but steady recovery under its new local management. The operating hours were immediately increased and passenger and freight traffic reflected this. Aircraft movements, and hence airport revenue, also became more buoyant, with, for example, operators of flying training schools using the excellent facilities and good weather record, particularly in the winter months. British Island Airways, Dan Air and Express Air Services were the main scheduled service operators, flying on routes to the Channel Islands and to the north of England in particular. The College of Air Training based its twin-engined aircraft for commercial pilot training at Hurn until the world-wide slump in airline operations reduced the demand for pilots. On the industrial side Flight Refuelling Ltd moved in with its flight test operations following the closure of Tarrant Rushton airfield near Blandford. This brought Canberras and Sea Vixens in various experimental guises for high-speed target towing and as 'drones'. Glos-Air expanded its aircraft sales and overhaul facilities, dealing especially with the Rockwell range of executive twin and single-engined Commander aircraft.

Encouraged by the growing success of the airport, the joint councils operating committee launched upon a major development programme for the early 1980s, an important feature of which was the construction of a new international passenger terminal building to replace the unsightly temporary structures which had been part of the scene for the previous 30 years. The road skirting the southern and western end of the airfield was diverted enabling the full length of the runway to be used for taking off and landing, giving an increase of 1,500ft, thereby removing the load penalties previously imposed on passenger aircraft. This resulted in an immediate increase in the number of major tour operators scheduling charter flights through Hurn, and in the summer of 1984 this constituted 15% more passengers.

Although the volume of traffic and passengers using Hurn has not yet reached the peak potential of the airport, the trend is such that the airport operation as a whole, is making a satisfactory trading surplus in excess of £300,000 per annum. Major efforts have been made to fill the gap left by the closure of the British Aerospace factory. At the time of writing no significant manufacturing company had moved in, but a number of smaller concerns such as

Above left:
In 1984 Hurn was the venue for a major airshow, which is to be repeated in 1986 under the auspices of International Air Tattoo.

Left:
Flight Refuelling operates a miscellany of aircraft including a Canberra TT18, F-100F Super-Sabre and Sea Vixen D3 seen here in August 1984.

Above:
Line-up of Michael Carlton's jet aircraft — Meteor NF11, Hunter and Jet Provost T52 at Hurn early in 1985.

Hurn Airport Services had commenced operations in the factory area. Glos Air also fell into hard times and following liquidation was purchased by Michael Carlton's Brencham Group, which quickly put it back on to a sound footing by early 1984. During that year Brencham also took over another ailing aircraft overhaul business — Shirlstar, which subsequently provided the accommodation for Glos Air Aircraft Painting Division. The same company also purchased a majority holding in Metropolitan Airways, the airline which operates the 'link-city' services pioneered by Dan Air. Initially flying Twin Otters, the airline standardised on Shorts 3-30s at the end of 1984.

With over 150 aircraft based at Bournemouth-Hurn Airport in 1985, it has one of the widest range of operations of any airport in the UK. The diversity of aircraft types to be seen includes Hunter One's veteran jet aircraft of the 1950s and 1960s, Wessex and Dauphin helicopters in support of the off-shore oil exploration, F-100 Super-Sabres, Falcons and Sea Vixens with Flight Refuelling Ltd, executive Cessna Citations and Beech Super King Airs with air charter firms, flying club/school training aircraft, the Bulldogs of Southampton University Air Squadron, transport aircraft in the colours of Middle East air arms on overhaul with Airwork Ltd and Hurn Airport Services, and Boeing 737s and Douglas DC9s of a host of charter airlines. Bournemouth-Hurn Airport shows that there is a valid place for a locally controlled and financed regional airport which can provide an excellent service to a wide range of operators and not become a financial liability to local ratepayers. *

The story of Bournemouth-Hurn Airport was compiled from material provided by W. H. Longhurst, Airport Director and R. C. B. Ashworth whose wartime history of Hurn was first published in Action Stations 5 *(by R. C. B. Ashworth; Patrick Stephens Ltd).*

No Strings Attached

Bryan Philpott

The annals of aviation history contain many stories of men and women, who have stared death in the face, yet against all odds, lived to tell the tale. Two such men are Flt Sgt Nicholas Alkemade and Flt Lt Ken Topaz, whose stories have a common bond, albeit separated by a period of 22 years and some three-and-a-half miles in height! They both saved their lives without their parachutes deploying.

In the case of Nicholas Alkemade his had no

chance to do so, since he left it behind when he abandoned his stricken Lancaster, and Ken Topaz's never left its pack because he was too low for it to operate.

On the evening of 25/26 March 1944 Flt Sgt Alkemade — a rear gunner — was briefed, with the rest of the crews of No 115 Squadron to take their Mk 11 Lancaster to Berlin. The squadron operated from Witchford and was the first unit to be totally equipped with the Hercules radial-engined Lancaster. Alkemade's aircraft was DS664, nicknamed 'Werewolf', and the trip marked the half-way stage (15 ops) of his tour.

Over Germany the Lancaster was attacked by

Below:
The vulnerable tail gunner's location can be clearly seen in this shot of a Lancaster. *John Dunnell*

a night-fighter, whose cannons set fire to the aircraft's main fuel tanks. Alkemade turned his turret along the axis of the aircraft, opened the twin doors, and reached for his chest type parachute which he had placed in its stowage prior to take-off. He was horrified to find the fuselage interior, including his parachute and its stowage rack ablaze, quickly slamming the doors closed, he rotated the turret and rather than face a slow death by burning opted for a quick clean end. Opening the doors he somersaulted backwards from the turret at a height of 18,000ft.

Fate now took a hand.

The flight sergeant fell into an isolated copse of pine trees, crashed through their branches, and had his fall cushioned by 18in of snow which had drifted beneath them. The area around this copse was completely free of other trees or snow, although the air gunner did not know this until daylight when he recovered consciousness. Apart from scratches and painful areas where pine needles had penetrated his skin, his only other injury was a twisted leg sustained when he left the aircraft.

His captors found the story somewhat hard to believe, but after examining his harness, which had clearly not been used, and finding the remains of his 'chute in the wrecked Lancaster, they realised that the fortunate gunner was telling the truth. Later on, a Luftwaffe colonel signed a document authenticating the escape and this was handed to Alkemade, thus giving him tangible proof that it was not just another story for the 'line-book'.

Some 22 years later, fate again intervened, but this time under entirely different circumstances, although the end result was remarkably similar. Flt Lt Ken Topaz was the Air Electronics Officer (AEO) of an ECM Canberra B2 (WH857) whose crew was briefed to carry out an exercise in the Yeovilton area on 3 May 1966. The Canberra, carrying a full fuel load including tip tanks, taxied to the end of the main runway at Watton, as the three crew members busied themselves with pre-take-off checks. It was a typical English spring day, the deep blue of the sky being enhanced by the yellow ball of the sun which had chased off all the early morning clouds. There was a slight crosswind, but nothing to cause the experienced pilot any concern, as he called for take-off clearance and swung the Canberra on to the centreline of the runway. At precisely 10.20 the aircraft was airborne, and as the Norfolk countryside slipped below, crew members reported that all systems were serviceable. The navigator, who incidentally, was a Canadian officer on an exchange posting, passed the first heading to the pilot, then settled back to savour

Above left:
Flt Lt Ken Topaz (top left) in front of an ECM Canberra B2 at Watton. *RAF Watton*

Below:
The wing tip tank was deposited on the perimeter track. *RAF Watton*

what was scheduled to be his last Canberra sortie before returning home.

As the aircraft departed Watton, part of the electronic equipment became unserviceable, and despite the efforts of the AEO, remained so. Without this piece of equipment there was no point in carrying on with the briefed sortie, so the captain advised air traffic at Watton that he was returning. Rather than make the whole trip abortive, the pilot decided to get some value from it by carrying out a Gee homing and let down, leading into an ACR 7 pickup.

As the Canberra approached the pickup point, the captain reduced power on the starboard engine to an idle position. This being a state where the power unit gave zero thrust and no drag. The objective being to carry out an asymmetric approach and landing. Contact with radar was established at five miles, and an approach to the runway was started. As the pilot and navigator exchanged the litany of normal pre-landing checks, the AEO started to shut-down his equipment and tighten his seat

Below:
Flt Lt Topaz's seat in the foreground with the navigator's beyond. *RAF Watton*

harness, a procedure he always adopted once the aircraft was on finals.

The radar talk-down continued until at one mile, the controller reported, 'Your are one mile from touch-down, look ahead and land visually.' At this point the AEO looked forward into the cockpit, and quite clearly saw the reflection of the lead-in lights on the inside of the canopy. Although he felt that this was unusual, he had not at that time flown many hours on Canberras and was prepared to accept it. Almost at the same time, the navigator sitting to the AEO's left, pointed to the ASI which was falling through 85kt, and the altimeter which was reading below 100ft.

At the weight the Canberra was flying, the speed across the hedge should have been something like 125kt, so it was very slow at this particular point of its approach. The two rear crew members said nothing, but suddenly noticed that full power was being applied to both engines. The 'live' one picked up immediately, the idling one seemed to catch, then surged, and probably flamed-out. The Canberra started to yaw sharply and rolled to starboard, the port wing came up to the almost vertical position, then the aircraft flick-rolled

very rapidly to port, and the wing tank hit the perimeter track just to the left of the runway. The Canberra cartwheeled about the port wing, eventually striking its nose on the ground and breaking off this section just forward of the main spar, coming to rest about 500yd from the point of first impact.

Above:
The AEO's unopened parachute pack. *RAF Watton*

Below:
The wrecked Canberra lay not far away. *RAF Watton*

It is perhaps not surprising that the AEO has no memory of his actual ejection from the aircraft; in fact he can only recall the wingtip striking the ground and then finding himself sitting on his parachute pack on the airfield.

In the B2 the rear seats were arranged side-by-side with the guide rails angled slightly away from each other to give sufficient crew separation. As both rear crew members ejected, the navigator's seat hit the frangible hatch first — the explosive bolts removing this had not been fired — and this attached itself to the top of his seat. The added weight and drag of the hatch prevented the navigator's seat from attaining any height, and he hit the ground with a high forward speed which caused serious injuries from which soon after he died. The angle of the guide rails, and the slightly delayed ejection of the AEO, coupled to the fact that as he was on the starboard side he was fired away from the angle of crash, gave him enough height to have a chance. The barostat on the seat, ran down very quickly, as would be expected at this low level, and separation from the seat occurred at zero forward speed with the occupant in a normal position. So in effect, he was deposited on his feet almost as though he had simply

stepped from the aircraft. The timing of the ejection, and the angle the seat made with the horizontal were, by good fortune, absolutely correct, it is doubtful if such a situation could ever be simulated.

Flt Lt Topaz's first recall after the aircraft started to roll, is sitting on the grass and putting his hand out to stop himself toppling off his still packed parachute. The Canberra was burning furiously some 50yd behind him, and the wind direction was such that it carried the smoke and flames away. The port engine bounced passed him and the GEE set thumped into the ground about a foot away. He undid his helmet and oxygen mask, took them off and looked around. He remembers:

'I was sitting there quite clear of it all, indeed one of the things I remember very strongly was looking round and seeing the airfield of Watton, certainly the spot I was in, absolutely covered in daisies; that is a very strong recollection in my mind. I sat surrounded by chaos for what seemed an eternity — but I doubt that it was. I checked the functions of my fingers and toes just in case I had back damage; everything seemed OK, but I decided not to stand as my legs were still a little numb. Eventually, in reality probably less than 30 seconds, a figure appeared — the station dentist I believe — he produced a sharp knife and despite my warnings about the destruction of service property, proceeded to cut me out of my parachute harness and Mae West (life jacket).'

The parameters of the Martin-Baker 1CN seat used by Flt Lt Topaz, were minima of 1,000ft and 125kt. As far as it is possible to ascertain he left the Canberra below 80kt and certainly well under 100ft, so it is not too surprising that at a subsequent dinner given by the Martin-Baker company to successful ejectees, Sir James Martin commented to him, 'I did not design that seat to do what you did with it my boy.'

Apart from a small scratch on his left ankle, Flt Lt Topaz suffered no injuries, but sadly both the navigator and pilot were killed. He went on to join the 'V' force and left the RAF in 1974.

USAF in Britain

Jeff Williams

United States Air Force aircraft have been flying from bases in Britain since 1942 and several of today's tactical units are descendants of those that were involved in the air war over Europe.

The present chapter of RAF-USAF co-operation is normally marked by the USAF's return to Britain in July 1948 as a result of the Berlin crisis — less than two years after the last WW2 unit had departed for the United States. The story really begins in January 1946, a time when most people had one thing on their minds — demobilisation. Two exceptions were US General Carl Spaatz and Air Marshal Sir Arthur Tedder, who were making a farewell trip to USAF bases in Britain about that time. Worried about the fully armed Soviet military force that stood ready in the East while the West disbanded, they wondered what would happen if the United States found it necessary to deploy its long range B-29s to Europe. Not a single British airfield was equipped to handle them. To correct this, they decided informally that the RAF would prepare four East Anglia bases to receive B-29s — just in case. The decision was a wise one.

The story of the Berlin Blockade of 1948 with its airlift of 2,343,315 tons of food and coal into the city by RAF and USAF planes is well known. Not so well publicised was the movement of Strategic Air Command B-29s into the fields that had been prepared for them. These USAF bombers — in conjunction with the striking power of the RAF — provided the West's answer to the powerful strength of the Red Army. They were a warning to the Soviets against pushing too far. And they were the beginning of a revived USAF build-up in the United Kingdom which has continued to this day.

These first bombers — arriving in July and August 1948 — were based at RAF Scampton, RAF Marham, RAF Waddington, and RAF Lakenheath. The Third Air Division (Provisional) was activated just prior to their arrival to prepare to receive, support, and operationally control these units on what was expected to be a 30 to 60 day temporary duty. It soon became apparent that this was not to be the case. On 23 August 1948 the provisional title was dropped and on 8 September the Third Air Division moved into quarters at South Ruislip.

From 1948 to 1950 all combat air units in the

Below:
Longest serving aircraft in the USAFE inventory is this RF-4C Phantom with the 10th TRW at RAF Alconbury. *Daniel March*

United Kingdom were under the operational control of the Third Air Division. Throughout this period Strategic Air Command bombers rotated for 90-day periods to UK bases — adding RAF Sculthorpe to the original four sites in eastern England. As evidence of Soviet truculence mounted, plans were made to build four new USAF bomber bases with the United States and Britain sharing costs. Because of the vulnerability of the East Anglian bases, it was decided to place the additional facilities behind the RAF fighter screen. After careful considera-

tion of several sites in England and Scotland, the two partners agreed that they would be located at Fairford, Greenham Common, Brize Norton and Upper Heyford. The arrangement for building these bases was covered by an 'Ambassadors Agreement' signed in April 1950 by the US Ambassador Lewis Douglas and the UK Under-Secretary for Air Aidan Crawley. They were to be available so long as the presence of USAF units in the country was 'considered desirable in the interests of common defense'.

Third Air Division continued to control USAF operations in Britain until early 1951, when Strategic Air Command (SAC) established the Seventh Air Division, assigning it the task of handling SAC operations at UK bases. Shortly thereafter the Third Air Division was deactivated, only to be replaced as the Third Air Force in May 1951 with the larger mission of

Below:
A 20th TFW F-111E climbing out from RAF Upper Heyford for a training mission.

Bottom:
This electronic countermeasures EF-111A 'Raven' was a newcomer to the UK in 1984, when it joined the 20th TFW. *Andrew March*

overseeing tactical operations from the UK and logistical support of the Seventh Air Division. This role continued until 1966 when the Seventh Air Division was deactivated.

The latest phase of the USAF's postwar history in Britain started in 1959, the year President DeGaulle placed limitations on US tactical forces in France. As a result, two front-line wings moved into Britain — the 10th Tactical Reconnaissance Wing to RAF Alconbury and the 48th Tactical Fighter Wing to RAF Lakenheath. Although not apparent at the time, this was but the first step in the total

withdrawal from France. In March 1966 the French Government made public its decision to withdraw from military participation in the North Atlantic Treaty Organisation (NATO) alliance. As a result, in mid-1966 the Third Air Force units in Britain were increased by the transfer from France of the 513th Troop Carrier Wing to RAF Mildenhall, the 66th Tactical Reconnaissance Wing to RAF Upper Heyford, and one additional squadron to the 10th Tactical Reconnaissance Wing at RAF Alconbury. Additionally, the 322nd Air Division, Military Airlift Command, moved to RAF High Wycombe. During the same period the tactical power of USAF units was increased by conversion from the F-101 Voodoo and RB-66 Destroyer to the F-4C and RF-4C Phantom.

In a USAFE reorganisation move in 1972, daily operational control of all USAFE units was transferred from the subordinate numbered

Below:
A formation take-off by a pair of A-10 Thunderbolts from the 81st TFW at Woodbridge. *Andrew March*

Bottom:
The ungainly A-10 is heavily armed and armoured for anti-tank duties in Europe.

Above left:
These Aggressor Squadron F-5E Tiger IIs are painted in the colour schemes of various Eastern bloc countries for combat training with NATO fighter aircraft.

Left:
Based in West Germany and Holland, F-15 Eagles like this example from Bitburg, are regular visitors to Alconbury for training with the Aggressor Tigers.

Below left:
Strategic Air Command established its first squadron of Lockheed TR-1 surveillance aircraft at RAF Alconbury in 1983. *Lockheed*

Above:
Mach 3 plus Lockheed SR-71s are regularly deployed to RAF Mildenhall.

air forces to Headquarters USAFE, and the Third Air Force headquarters was reduced in size and moved from South Ruislip to RAF Mildenhall, Suffolk.

Today, the commander of the Third Air Force, a major general, exercises command over USAFE tactical and support units in the UK; serves as the 'single point of contact' representing US forces in negotiating technical and financial arrangements with the British Government; and provides area support for all US forces in the UK.

The Third Air Force consists of six tactical wings, eight main operating bases and two standby deployment bases kept in readiness for contingency or wartime use. It involves

some 25,000 USAF men and women.

Main operating bases include RAF Lakenheath in Suffolk, with four squadrons of General Dynamics F-111F all-weather strike aircraft in the 48th Tactical Fighter Wing. These F-111Fs are due to be replaced by F-15E Eagles during 1986. Three additional squadrons of F-111Es and one squadron of EF-111A 'Ravens' make up the 20th Tactical Fighter Wing at RAF Upper Heyford, Oxfordshire.

The 81st Tactical Fighter Wing at the dual bases of RAF Bentwaters and RAF Woodbridge, Suffolk has six squadrons of Fairchild A-10 Thunderbolt II close air support aircraft. Military Airlift Command's 67th Aerospace Rescue and Recovery Squadron, with Sikorsky HH-53 Super Jolly helicopters and Lockheed HC-130 Hercules, is also located at RAF Woodbridge.

At RAF Alconbury, Cambridgeshire, the 10th Tactical Reconnaissance Wing is composed of a squadron of McDonnell Douglas RF-4C Phantom tactical reconnaissance aircraft and the 527th Tactical Fighter Training 'Aggressor' Squadron which flies Northrop F-5E Tiger II aircraft to provide dissimilar air combat training to other fighter units in Europe. SAC's 17th Tactical Reconnaissance Wing also operates the Lockheed TR-1 aircraft from Alconbury.

RAF Mildenhall is the 'Gateway to the United Kingdom' for USAF personnel arriving for a tour of duty here. The host 513th Tactical

Airlift Wing operates Boeing EC-135 command and control aircraft for US Commander in Chief Europe and provides support for a rotational squadron of Lockheed C-130 Hercules, rotational Boeing KC-135 Stratotankers and transient Lockheed C-5 Galaxy, Lockheed C-141 Starlifter and other transport aircraft.

The 7020th Air Base Group at RAF Fairford, Gloucestershire, provides support for rotational KC-135 Stratotankers operated by the 11th Strategic Group and the 7274th Air Base Group at RAF Chicksands, Bedfordshire, provides support for the Electronic Security Command's 6950th Electronic Security Group.

RAF Greenham Common, hosting the 501st Tactical Missile Wing, has the ground launched cruise missile (GLCM). RAF Sculthorpe in Norfolk and RAF Wethersfield in Essex are standby deployment bases. RAF Wethersfield is the home of Detachment 1, 10th Tactical

Reconnaissance Wing and the 819th Civil Engineering Squadron (Red Horse). RAF Sculthorpe hosts Detachment 1, 48th Tactical Fighter Wing.

How does this impressive force fit into the present NATO structure

Operational command over all US forces in Europe is exercised by the US Commander-in-Chief Europe (USCINCEUR), a US Army general who is also SACEUR and reports directly to the Joint Chiefs of Staff in Washington. His headquarters is the United States European Command (USEUCOM) in Stuttgart, Germany.

The United States Air Forces in Europe (USAFE), with headquarters at Ramstein Air Base, Germany, is organised into three numbered air forces, the Third, Sixteenth and Seventeenth. USAFE aircraft earmarked for

Top left:
The giant Lockheed C-5 Galaxy is employed by Military Airlift Command to provide an air-bridge between the USA and Europe through RAF Mildenhall. *Lockheed*

Above left:
Looking unusual in 'warpaint' this C-141B Starlifter is another transport aircraft regularly seen at Mildenhall.

Top:
Delivering freight in the field (here using the Low Altitude Parachute Extraction System) is a task for the C-130H Hercules of the 513th Tactical Airlift Wing. *Lockheed*

Above:
KC-135 Stratotankers visit the UK on 30-day rotations from the USA to provide aerial refuelling, based at Mildenhall and Fairford. *Andrew March*

NATO use in time of war constitute the largest single air contribution of any nation in the Alliance.

USAFE is a component command of USEU-COM and a major command of the United States Air Force. In addition, the Commander-in-Chief of USAFE (CINCUSAFE) functions in a NATO role as Commander, Allied Air Forces Central Europe (COMAAFCE).

In peacetime, USAFE trains and equips US Air Force units pledged to NATO, maintaining combat-ready units dispersed in an area from the United Kingdom to Turkey. The command not only provides fighter, reconnaissance and airlift support for all major NATO exercises conducted in the Western European area but also assists air forces of other NATO nations to develop their combat capabilities.

USAFE is composed of more than 60,000 military men and women who fly, maintain and support more than 790 tactical aircraft, including tactical fighter, reconnaissance, forward air control and command and control types.

633 Squadron's Mosquitos

Robert Rudhall

Twenty-two years ago this year film-makers immortalised one of Britain's best known and best loved aeroplanes of World War 2, the de Havilland Mosquito, but sadly at the expense of three examples of the wooden wonder.

The war film '633 Squadron' went on general release in British cinemas in 1964. To the ordinary cinema-goer, the most memorable part of the film will probably be the stirring theme music written by the prolific film music composer, Ron Goodwin. But to the aircraft enthusiast the main draw was the de Havilland Mosquito aircraft which featured in the film.

The principal airfield sequences were filmed at RAF Bovingdon. In fact in some shots eagle-eyed observers can make out RAF Anson's and Pembrokes parked on the far side of the airfield. The Norwegian fjord scenes were filmed in Scotland, which entailed some very low flying from the Mosquitos and the B-25 Mitchell camera plane.

In terms of airworthy Mosquitos, the film was made at just the right time. Never again would five flyable Mosquitos be available in the same place at the same time. Four more Mosquitos were used in the film of which three were able to taxi and the fourth was used as 'static dressing'.

In overall charge of the airworthy aircraft was the late Capt John Crewdson of Film Aviation Services. Flying one of the Mosquitos was John

Jeff Hawke, who at that time was a flight lieutenant in the RAF and has since become involved with many aircraft used for film work, including flying the Mitchell camera plane for the 'Battle of Britain', flying a Dakota in 'A Bridge Too Far' and the task of organising the flight across the Atlantic of five B-25 Mitchells for the film 'Hanover Street'.

The airworthy Mossies were RS709, RS712, TA639, TA719 and TW117, of which RS709 and RS712 were Airspeed-built B35s converted to TT35s. TA639 and TA719 were de Havilland (Hatfield)-built B35s converted to TT35s. TW117 was a de Havilland (Leavesden)-built TIII.

RS709 ex-No 3 CAACU (Civilian Anti-Aircraft Co-operation Unit) based at Exeter,

Below:
No 633 Squadron Mosquito demonstrating its film performance. *Andrew March*

Top right:
Mosquito TT35 TA719 served with No 3 CAACU at Exeter, like most of the other aircraft, prior to the filming

Right:
Modified and painted as a B35 TA719 was used for much of the solo filming.

Below right:
Unfortunately TA719 crashed at Staverton in 1964 and was stored in a damaged condition. *Roger Wasley*

which was given the civil registration G-ASKA. After filming it was flown to its new home at the Skyfame Aircraft Museum, Staverton Airport, where it stayed for several years before being used in the sequel film to '633 Squadron' in 1968. It was then sold and eventually flown across the Atlantic to join the ranks of the Confederate Air Force. After several years RS709 came back to Britain, to Doug Arnold at Blackbushe where it was carefully restored for its latest owners, the USAF Museum: in the autumn of 1984 went back to the USA but was grounded at Goose Bay, Labrador for some months with engine problems.

TT35 RS712/G-ASKB was purchased after filming by Grp Capt 'Hamish' Mahaddie (who a few years later was responsible for gathering together all the aircraft used in the film 'Battle of Britain'). RS712 was stored for several years at West Malling, Kent until the mid-1970s when it was acquired by Sir William Roberts for his Strathallan Aircraft Museum. It was refurbished and put back into its original silver-doped finish

and was flown several times at Strathallan by the late Neil Williams. In 1981 it was included in the Christies Auction at Strathallan, and was sold for £100,000 to the American collector Kermit Weeks. It remained in Scotland for several years until prepared for its trans-Atlantic trip by Personal Plane Services at Booker early in 1985.

TA639 was retained by the RAF and after filming it was based for a while at RAF Little Rissington, where it made several flights. After being grounded it was transferred to the Aerospace Museum at RAF Cosford, where it remains on display to the public.

TA719/G-ASKC had been purchased just before filming commenced by the Skyfame Museum at Staverton. It was made available to

Above:
Hatfield-built TA639 has been retained by the RAF and is displayed in the Cosford Aerospace Museum.

Below:
RS709 was owned by the Skyfame Museum and also used for the sequel to '633 Squadron . . .'

Above:
...before being sold to the USA as N9797 in 1968.

Below:
Owned by the Imperial War Museum, after filming Mosquito T3 TV959 was put on display at Lambeth minus its starboard wing.

the film company, and in fact TA719 was the aircraft that was the subject of most filming, being used for almost all of the film's solo Mosquito scenes.

After filming was over TA719 flew to Staverton where Skyfame kept it airworthy for demonstrations, until an unfortunate 'dead stick' landing in the autumn of 1964. The aircraft was partially restored for static display and remained with Skyfame until the Museum moved to Duxford during January 1978, and a full restoration to exhibition standard is now well advanced.

TW117 remained on RAF charge and after the film was completed it was put into storage for a number of years until the opening of the Royal Air Force Museum at Hendon in 1972, when it was put on display in the standard trainer scheme of silver overall with yellow bands around the wings and fuselage. It has since been moved into the Bomber Command Museum next door to the main RAF Museum. Of the three aircraft that were able only to taxi, less happier fates were in store. TA642, A TT35, was to have been used in the sequence where the shot-up Mosquito returns to base and makes a wheels up landing. But the gremlins took a hand and in a normal taxying sequence during filming, the undercarriage folded up by itself. The aircraft was damaged beyond repair, and was used later in the studio for filming inside the cockpit. Another Mosquito was brought in for the crash-landing scene. This was RS718, another TT35, which was taxied by John

Crewdson at high speed across the airfield and the undercarriage retracted for the cameras. Another TT35, TA724 met its end even more dramatically when it was taxied with the aid of a control line arrangement into a fuel bowser during the air raid sequence; the ensuing explosion destroyed both the Mosquito and the fuel bowser.

The remaining aircraft, TV959, a Leavesden-built TIII, along with the nose section of TT35 TJ118, was used for filming actors in the cockpit. TV959 belonged to the Imperial War Museum and was put on display at South Lambeth, suspended from the ceiling minus its starboard outer wing. The wing section is reported to be in store at the IWM Duxford and, it is hoped that one day the two parts will be reunited and displayed as a complete aircraft again.

'633 Squadron' was a success at the box office, so much so that a sequel was made in 1968 called 'Mosquito Squadron'. By 1968 the number of Mosquitos available was depleted somewhat and a lot of footage from '633 Squadron' was used in place of new filming. '633 Squadron' was made in the nick of time. Our film record of the wooden wonder is all the better for the efforts that went into its making.

Adrian Gjertsen looping *Hunter One* G-HUNT high over Dorset for the camera of Arthur Gibson.